THE BIG
FIGHT

★ ★

CHRISTIAN MEN VS THE WORLD, FLESH & DEVIL

thegoodbook
COMPANY

The Big Fight
Christian Men versus the World, the Flesh and the Devil
© The Good Book Company 2012

Published by
The Good Book Company
Tel (UK): 0333-123-0880;
International: +44 (0) 208 942 0880
Email: admin@thegoodbook.co.uk

thegoodbook
COMPANY

Websites:
UK: www.thegoodbook.co.uk
North America: www.thegoodbook.com
Australia: www.thegoodbook.com.au
New Zealand: www.thegoodbook.co.nz

ISBN: 9781908317865

Cover design: André Parker/Ninefootone Creative
Printed and bound by CPI Group (UK) Ltd, Croydon, CR0 4YY

Contents

T he flashbulbs were going all around him, and the
noise was incredible. A roaring tide of sound that
made it impossible for him to hear what was being
shouted in his ear as he climbed through the ropes.

He was pushed and pulled onto the hard wooden stool.
Someone was rubbing his shoulders, and giving stinging
slaps to his bare skin, preparing him for what was to come.
Another guy he had not met before was pulling at the strings
on his gloves in a workmanlike way, not daring to look in his
eyes.

There was a sad determination about the cornermen that
scared him. These guys knew in detail what was about to
happen to him, in a way he could only guess. But the man
knew he wouldn't have to guess for much longer.

There was a renewed frenzy as the roar rose in pitch, and
another explosion of flashes from the cameras. The ropes
parted to let in the Adversary.

As the man caught sight of the Adversary, his ears were

suddenly deaf to the noise, as his guts did a somersault. It felt like his courage and resolve had turned to liquid, and drained out through a hole in his heart.

The man on the other side of the ring was simply enormous.

His muscles bulged and rippled. His biceps looked like iron. His fists great clubs that would soon be pounding him senseless.

But that wasn't what frightened him the most.

It was the look of snarling contempt and hatred that filled every part of his face, and the eyes that bored into him like a drill. It was a look that said loud and clear: "You are dead meat—and I'm going to butcher you".

The man shambled through the formalities in a daze. The echoing announcements were barely comprehensible. His head was low and he didn't dare look into that face again, for fear that he would turn and run. The only thought in his head was: "How can I get out of this?"

"Shake hands, and when the bell sounds, come out of your corner fighting." The familiar words had never sounded more like the last rites.

Still quavering, he returned to the corner. The team crowded round. A last swish of water in his bone-dry mouth. The gum shield shoved roughly in place.

And then he was all alone under the searing lights in a sea of noise which rose to a frenzy as a distant bell sounded.

This was it...

This is a book for men who are involved in the greatest fight of all time. It's a daily struggle that anyone who has put their faith in Christ is involved in. It's a fight against three hostile and powerful opponents: the world, the flesh and the devil.

This is a book written *by* men, specifically *for* men. That's not to say that women are non-combatants in this war. They are fighting the same fight. But many of the battles are also subtly different because of the way we are put together. We wanted to express some insights from the Bible and from our own experience to specifically help men engage with the particular battles they face.

Let's be honest

And the first step towards that is some ruthless honesty about the *nature* of the fight. Men are often less able to talk about the deep things they are struggling with. And instinctively, men feel they ought to be able to deal with it on their own. We think it is manly to "do it yourself".

Not so.

The flesh: The Bible tells us that our fallen inner desires wage war daily against the new life that Christ has planted in our souls. And they just refuse to go away.

The devil: The Bible tells us that we have a powerful spiritual enemy in Satan, who prowls around like a roaring lion seeking someone to devour. It tells us he is the father of lies and only wants to kill and destroy. His timely temptations and whispered accusations threaten to derail us at every turn.

The world: As men of God we are called to live and work in a fallen world. But that world is constantly trying to squeeze us into its own way of thinking. Anyone who wants to follow Christ knows that it is hard to be constantly swimming against the tide of opinion and lifestyle. But that is what we are called to do. To show the difference that belonging to Jesus makes as we live out our lives in ordinary ways.

Some of the battles are obvious—against pride, porn– ography and the lure of riches and comfort. Others are more subtle and can get to us "under the radar". If you know you are struggling with a specific issue, we hope and pray that you will find help here. But it may be that this book will also awaken you to something that you were unaware of. As you read it, be prepared to be honest about where you are at in *The Big Fight*.

No magic bullet

We want to be *realistic* about the struggles that men face on a daily basis, but we also want to be *practical* about the way we fight. There is no knock-out punch that will end this war for a Christian man this side of the grave. No magic bullet to fire. But what we have tried to express in the following pages will make all the difference, because the Christian man will arm himself for this fight, not with techniques or clever strategies, but with the truth of the gospel.

That's why the Bible is at the centre of this book. As we open its pages, we discover it is like a mirror—it strips away the false heroic image we have of ourselves, and shows us as we truly are. Weak and helpless sinners in need of a Saviour. Wayward and ungrateful children in need of a loving Father's discipline. Proud and self-reliant rebels who need the power of the Holy Spirit in our lives to transform our hearts, and the caring company of other believers to help us keep going.

But the Scriptures show us far more than our need. They reveal to us the unfolding plan of our loving God, who sent His Son to die so that we might find forgiveness. Who raised

His Son from the dead so that we might have new life. Who sent His Holy Spirit so that Jesus' life would grow in us and in our churches. And it is this gospel that we must apply to our hearts, lives and struggles if we are not to be crushed by the assault of these fearsome enemies.

The final bell

Because, fierce as it is, we need to understand that this is a battle in which the *outcome is already known.* Complete and utter victory for Jesus Christ and those who belong to Him. A devastating, total and crushing defeat for the world, the flesh and the devil.

All of human history, and our individual lives, are moving towards the day when that victory will be revealed for all the world to see. But although the war has been won by our Captain, the enemy remains dangerous. The battles we face as individual Christians now are part of a desperate rearguard action by an enemy that knows it is defeated. They are the twitching corpse-like reactions of the "old me", who has died with Christ. They are the struggles of those who have chosen the narrow way to life, but who daily live with those who are cruising a broad path that leads to destruction.

Our victory with Christ is assured—we just need to keep going until the final bell. Jesus tells us: "Be faithful, even to the point of death, and I will give you the crown of life"[1].

And God has given us all the resources we need to keep going to the end. In many ways this book is simply a reminder to you to make use of all the resources He has given us in the gospel.

---

1 Revelation 2 v 10

Ways to use this book

There are a number of ways in which you can use this book to help you.

1. If you are struggling with one particular issue, **just turn to the chapter** and use the resources to help you think through what your next step is. We hope you will find comfort in the stories of others who are struggling with the same issues, light from heaven in the Bible passages, and some practical pointers on what to do next.

2. You could read the book with a group of other men from your church or in your workplace, and meet to read the Bible together, to discuss and to pray for one another. This is a great way to grapple with the issues at the heart of *The Big Fight*, and you will find you are not fighting alone.

3. Hey—novel idea—you could read it on your own, and reflect on how these things apply to your own life, and where God is challenging you to grow.

However you use it, you should use it *prayerfully*. Talk to the Lord about the things you are battling with. Ask for His strength, and use the resources He has already given you: the assurance of your full and free forgiveness in Christ; the joy of being part of a band of brothers; the privilege of being an adopted child of God—a new creation in Christ; a mind being renewed by the Spirit of God; and the comfort and encouragement of God's word.

And pray that, in turn, you would be a help to other brothers who are struggling, because we never need to struggle alone. We are called to "carry each other's burdens and ... you will fulfil the law of Christ".[2]

---

2   Galatians 6 v 2

How do I deal with the memory of the things I have done?

Richard Coekin

> *"My guilt has overwhelmed me like a burden too heavy to bear." Psalm 38 v 4*

A young man came to see me recently who was emotionally paralysed by dreadful feelings of guilt. He's a Christian who's just married a terrific girl. But he confessed that he's still addicted to hard-core porn.

Like the psalmist above, his guilt was overwhelming him "like a burden too heavy to bear". Perhaps we all know something of such guilt for various failures of our own?

What should I say?

> *"Don't expect sympathy from me. You're guilty of disgusting sin and you're a disgrace to Jesus, so stop it!"*

Or perhaps instead,

> *"Hey, stop persecuting yourself. Many guys find it hard to kick the porn habit. Just remember that you're not guilty because you're forgiven by Jesus. Relax."*

Which is better? Is he right to feel guilty or not? What does God say about our guilt in the Bible?

The Bible teaches that we're **all guilty** of breaking God's laws. Breaking a law may not be serious if it's an "unwritten law" like not singing loudly on a train. Such guilt only suffers the mild penalty of threatening looks from fellow-passengers.

It's more serious if we're found guilty of breaking government laws like punching a traffic officer. We could find ourselves in prison. But it's *incredibly serious* when we're habitually guilty of breaking God's laws like loving God with all our heart, soul, mind and strength and loving our neighbours as ourselves.

Unless we're pardoned, the Bible says we'll be sentenced by God to permanent exclusion from His blessing in heaven to suffer His punishment in hell. The Bible warns that God will "not leave the guilty unpunished" on the day "when God will judge men's secrets through Jesus Christ, as my gospel declares" (Exodus 34 v 7; Romans 2 v 16). Being guilty of breaking God's law has dreadful eternal consequences.

God's love

Yet, amazingly, although we're all guilty of breaking His laws, God still passionately loves us. He's done something marvellous so that we can be declared "not guilty". The Bible declares that Christ our King "was delivered over to death for our sins and was raised to life for our justification" (Romans 4 v 25).

This means that Christ our King shrank Himself down to become an ordinary man like us (but never guilty of sin) in order to *swap* places with us on the cross. As our representative King, He was treated like us (guilty) so that we can be treated like Him (innocent). He was punished with degrading and agonising exclusion in hell on the cross, so that we are welcomed by God as His perfect sons and heirs.

We know that this swap works because Jesus was then raised from the dead, and exalted to heaven, proving that the life He lived for us was accepted into heaven. Let me illustrate with a story.

Three apprentices

Imagine that a respected and successful factory manager selected three of his young apprentices to enrol on his year-long management training programme. There was **Matt** *(able but rather too fond of going to clubs and dating women)*, **Phil** *(also gifted but annoyingly rebellious)* and **Chris** *(the manager's own son)*.

"Right lads," explained the manager on the first day of the programme. "I'm giving you each a box-file with your name on it. During the year I want you to fill this file with reports and studies prepared in your own time that record all that you're learning this year in a presentable format. At the end of the year, any of you without a completed folder of 500 pages of carefully presented reports will be thrown off this course. Are we clear? Good luck gentlemen!"

You can predict how the year progressed. Clubbing Matt came to work each Monday morning bleary-eyed and exhausted but with nothing to add to his folder. Rebellious Phil came to work muttering about how ridiculous the manager was and hardly a scrap for his folder.

The manager's son Chris quietly began to accumulate well-prepared reports for his Dad. He tried to persuade Matt and Phil to get started. He offered to help them. But they kept insisting that they'd catch up soon. But they never did, and as the year-end approached, it was clearly too late.

Matt swore he'd work all night through the last weekend, but his mates dragged him out to a party. Phil had given up bothering—he knew he'd blown it. They both turned up at work on the Monday expecting to be sacked.

To their enormous surprise, Matt and Phil walked in to find the manager returning their box-files to their desks with approving smiles. "Well done lads! To be honest I'm rather surprised, but this is outstanding work and I have high hopes for your futures." Turning to his son Chris, however, he was clearly very angry. "Chris, you've totally let me down. This work is an utter disgrace. Now get out—I'm a man of my word and you must go!"

As Chris left the building he winked mysteriously at Matt and Phil, who were too stunned to speak. But when they opened their files, they both found beautifully illustrated and immaculately prepared reports and studies, clearly all Chris's own work. And on their desks a short note for each of them:

"Thought you could do with a hand. All the best, Chris."

Having done their work for them, the manager's son had borne the penalty for their failures.

Actually, the story has a happy ending. Three days later, the manager discovered what had happened. He was so impressed with Chris that he invited him back as Managing Director. And Matt and Phil have been happy to work for him ever since!

This story illustrates how Christ, having lived the innocent life we haven't lived, then suffered the penalty for our guilt, and why the Father raised Him to heaven and why Christians are so glad to work for Him. We can now make four simple observations about our guilt today:

1. Many men don't feel guilty before God when they should!

The Psalmist observed:

> An announcement is within my heart concerning the
> sinfulness of the wicked: there is no fear of God before his
> eyes. For in his own eyes he flatters himself too much to
> detect or hate his sin.   **Psalm 36 v 1-2**

Many men don't seek the Saviour because they don't fear
God as they should because they don't feel guilty enough
about their sin.

2. Many religious men feel guilty before God about things that aren't wrong!

The Apostle Paul also warns us about false teachers who:

> forbid people to marry and order them to abstain from certain
> foods, which God created to be received with thanksgiving.
>   **1 Timothy 4 v 3**

Many men are taught by human religions to feel guilty
about thoroughly good things like getting married or eating
certain food or other blessings from God eg: the food laws
of Judaism, the fasting laws of Islam or the vows of Roman
Catholic monks.

3. Many men rightly feel guilty before God when His Spirit is convicting them of their need for the Saviour!

Jesus said:

> When he [the Holy Spirit] comes, he will convict the world of
> guilt in regard to sin and righteousness and judgment...
>   **John 16 v 8**

This means that Jesus' Holy Spirit continues to convict us through the Scriptures of our guilt under God's law, to show us our need of Him. This is our experience when we're becoming Christians and throughout our lives as Christians. Our awareness of guilt is an encouraging sign of the Holy Spirit's ministry in our lives. But His ministry doesn't end with guilt.

4. Christian men shouldn't keep feeling guilty because we are cleansed from our guilt by Jesus' blood!

The letter to the Hebrews says:

> let us draw near to God with a sincere heart in full assurance of faith, having our hearts sprinkled to cleanse us from a guilty conscience.
>
> **Hebrews 10 v 22**

He's been explaining that, like a high priest entering God's presence with the blood of a sacrifice for the sins of his people, Jesus has *permanently* entered God's presence in heaven as our High Priest with the sacrifice of His own blood shed for our sins on the cross. This means that the way is now open for us to live for ever in the presence of God **without guilt**, if we are "sprinkled" with Jesus' blood through trusting in His death for our sins.

Let me illustrate with a simple bathroom product. I use a shower gel which happens to be red when it comes out of the bottle, but turns white when used in the shower to scrub me clean. Whenever I use it, I'm reminded that when we put our trust in Christ we are "sprinkled" with Jesus' blood, and so our consciences are washed clean of all guilt before God. We can draw near to God, with a clear conscience that is free of guilt because we are men who have "showered" in the shed blood of Jesus.

In practice

So how do these gospel principles affect what I advised the young man paralysed by guilt about his hard-core porn addiction?

Firstly, **he's right to feel guilty** for offending God with his lust. Our sin is serious.

Second, **he's not guilty of wanting sex**. It's a good desire that has been distorted by sin. He needs to invest in his relationship with his wife, so that intimacy with her becomes more satisfying for him than the twisted excitement he has been gaining from porn.

Third, **the Holy Spirit in him is convicting him of his sin and his need of the Saviour.** In this sense, his guilt is good news. God has not given up on him, but is provoking him to repent, and showing him that he needs to look to Christ for forgiveness and the resources to deal with his addiction.

Fourth, Christ loves him so much that, having lived a lust-free life for us, Christ fully suffered the penalty for his porn addiction on the cross so that **he is "not guilty" before God any longer.**

That's why Jesus was exalted. And that's why we love Jesus more than lust. That's why we pray for His strength to dry up the river of porn, and our desire for it. That might involve installing a computer "Net-Nanny". It will involve seeking God's strength from the fellowship of other Christian men who can encourage him. It will involve telling his wife to seek her forgiveness, understanding and help. But most of all, it will involve reminding himself that the cleansing blood of Jesus has washed him clean so that he is not guilty any longer.

Robert: *"Guilt is good..."*

When I first became a Christian as a student, there was an incredible feeling of being forgiven by Jesus. But a few months on, it all started to fall apart.

I read in the Bible about how God hates stealing. Before I was a Christian, I had done some casual shoplifting. Small stuff. Nothing to put me in prison, and probably unnoticed or long forgotten by the shops themselves. But as I read God's word, I knew that real repentance meant I had to put it right. But, for various reasons, I convinced myself that it didn't matter, so I put it out of my mind.

Mercifully, God doesn't give up that easily.

I began to feel more and more guilty about it until my life was a misery. In the end, I turned to God and asked for his help to genuinely repent. The next weekend I hand-delivered envelopes to the managers at three shops in my home town with money, and a personal note explaining what it was all about. *Job done.*

I've seen that pattern repeated a number of times in my life, over things which might be considered much more serious. Sometimes I have needed the help of Christian friends to point out the stupidity of my ways.

Although I hate to feel guilty, I know that it's a sign that God has not abandoned me. It's a sign that His Holy Spirit continues to wrestle with the "old me". It's a sign that I am God's son, and that He is disciplining me, and provoking me to grow. Contrary to what the world thinks, *true guilt is a good thing*.

I have known some Christian brothers who have very sensitive consciences. They are sometimes dealing with false guilt, which *is* a bad thing—endlessly agonising over things that they can do nothing about, and feeling wretched about them. At heart it shows a lack of trust in God's forgiveness. Sometimes we believe the devil's whispered accusations. I've sometimes needed to tell them to just "stop worrying, trust Jesus and get on with life".

I, however, am in danger of the opposite extreme. I am too often hard hearted about sins I need to hate in myself. So I try to pray that God would point things out in my life that I need to work on.

It's an uncomfortable prayer to pray. But it leads to the kind of guilt that I know is good for me. Guilt that leads me to repent, grow and be filled with joy as I experience again God's love and forgiveness for me.

Bible study

Read Psalm 32

- v 1-2: *How can sinners like us be blessed?*

- v 3-6: *How can we be relieved of our guilt every day?*

- v 6-7: *When do we most urgently need to pray?*

- v 8-10: *Why should we stop stubbornly resisting God's instruction?*

- v 11: *How will we find joy in the LORD throughout our lives?*

Discuss

- *What things make you feel guilty?*
  Should you feel guilty about them or not?

- *How does the world affect our view of guilt?*

- *How do the devil's lies affect our view of guilt?*

- *How does our sinful flesh affect our view of guilt?*

- *How does the word of God affect our view of guilt?*

- *How does the gift of the Spirit affect our feelings of guilt?*

- *How does the death of Jesus Christ affect our feelings of guilt?*

- *What would you say to someone who confessed their feelings of guilt over unduly harsh words spoken to a friend?*

Further help

You can change, Tim Chester (IVP).
The vanishing conscience, John MacArthur (Thomas Nelson).

Why do I find it so hard to be generous with my time and money?

Matt Fuller

I've just moved house and I'm struggling with issues about money. Moving house is expensive. Windows need curtains, walls need paint, and rooms need furniture. We could make do with a 20-year-old sofa, although it would be nice to have a new one.

And I'm wondering: "How much money is it okay to spend on this stuff?" Even asking the question makes me realise I'm a lot older and more dull than I used to be.

Of course, that may not be your issue with money at all. Yet the curious thing about money is that it can encourage a broad range of sinful attitudes. As Paul reminds us:

The love of money is a root of all kinds of evil. **1 Tim 6 v 10**

Money doesn't discriminate: you can love it if you are rich with lots, or if you are poor with none.

It's worth picking out three sinful attitudes which money can produce:

1. If I have money… it's because I'm impressive!

If you have a good income or are comfortably off it's very easy to become proud. Deuteronomy 8 is a great chapter on the danger of self-satisfied pride:

> You may say to yourself, "My power and the strength of my hands have produced this wealth for me." But remember the Lord your God, for it is he who gives you the ability to produce wealth.
> **Deuteronomy 8 v 17-18**

Naturally, it's easy to think: "I've worked hard for my money, my success, my house, and it's all mine." We need to be humbled by the truth that God has given us our abilities and opportunities in life. Being born in the UK gives me many advantages that being born in Afghanistan does not. And that was God's choice, not mine.

Herbert Smith is a Nobel-prize-winning economist. His research was into the impact of social capital. Social capital is made up of things such as a stable democratic government, natural resources, and technological skills in the community. These are the foundation upon which the rich can begin their work.

He estimated that 90% of what people earn in wealthy "western" societies is down to social capital. Wow! This means that just 10% of your "success" is down to you. A whopping 90% is down to the country in which you are born and the opportunities available.

Warren Buffett, the American billionaire investor, was so impressed with this research that he has committed to give away 90% of his income before he dies. He put it nicely:

> *If you stick me down in the middle of Bangladesh or Peru in the nineteenth century, you'll quickly find out how much this talent is going to produce in the wrong soil.*

Deuteronomy 8 is even clearer.

- *You've earned money because of your quick brain?*
  The Lord gave you that brain.!
- *You're able to put in long hours at your job?*
  The Lord gave you that stamina!
- *You're a great networker?*
  The Lord gave you your character!
- *You've made a great scientific discovery?*
  The Lord gave you your education!
- *What have you got that the Lord did not give you?*
  Absolutely nothing!

What should we do in response?

> When you have eaten and are satisfied, praise the Lord your
> God for the good land he has given you.
>
> **Deuteronomy 8 v 10**

2. If I have money... then I'll be secure

I know some Christians who earn a lot of money, but who have very modest houses, and a very modest lifestyle. However, they seem to give away relatively little to Christian work. Where is the money going? The answer is often that they have massive savings. In moments of honesty they'll admit: "Sometimes I get really stressed, but then I look at our bank statements and calm down again."

Here then is the sin of thinking that money provides security, rather than trusting the Lord. It shouldn't take much to remind us how foolish that is!

> Command those who are rich in this present world not to
> be arrogant nor to put their hope in wealth, which is so

uncertain, but to put their hope in God, who richly provides
us with everything for our enjoyment.   **1 Timothy 6 v 17**

The Russian billionaire, Roman Abramovich, is a fabulously
wealthy man. The downside is that he is reportedly paranoid
about security. He has a private army of 40 former "Special
Ops" soldiers as bodyguards, costing millions every year. He
has installed on his private yacht a radar-guided anti-missile
defence system. Even if a missile did get through, the yacht
has a mini submarine to escape in an emergency.

Surely he's safe?

Well, maybe from being kidnapped. Yet in the same
month that his private yacht was launched, he collapsed
with a heart problem and was rushed to hospital. Can you
ever have enough money to make you "safe"?

We mere mortals might think Abramovich is odd. Yet do
you find yourself thinking: "We need more money in the
bank to be secure; we haven't got enough savings. If I just
had one month's salary in the bank I would feel safer... If I
just had one year's salary..."?

Don't misunderstand me. I'm not advocating a failure to
plan financially. The Bible praises the prudent ant that stores
up supplies (see Proverbs 30 v 24-25). There is little problem
with having thousands of pounds in the bank as long as you
don't place your hope in the money.

However, what makes you feel safe? Is your hope in money
or is it in the Lord?

3. If I have money... then I'll be content

Another way that we can put our faith in wealth is by
believing that it will bring contentment. We tell ourselves
that If only we had a little bit more money, then we would be
content. It's a lie. I was struck a number of years ago by this
editorial in *The Economist*:

Affluent countries have not grown happier as they have grown richer... Capitalism is adept at turning luxuries into necessities, bringing to the masses what the elites have always enjoyed, but the flip side of this genius is that people come to take for granted things they once coveted from afar... People are stuck on a treadmill: as they achieve a better standard of living, they become inured to its pleasures.

The treadmill is such a helpful metaphor. When you run on a treadmill, you go nowhere but reduce yourself to sweaty exhaustion (a personal testimony). We can exhaust ourselves chasing just a little bit more.

Money is the drug that can never satisfy. We *never* have enough to make us content. We tell ourselves: "I'm not like those silly people who play the lottery and think that becoming a millionaire is the answer to life. I only need a *little* bit more."

I was sent a funny *YouTube* clip recently of a man begging with his daughter on his lap. He was holding a piece of cardboard on which he had written: "Please help, I need money to upgrade my iphone." It's an accurate satire.

Things that were once deemed luxuries in our lives can quickly become "necessities" that we cannot imagine living without. As we grow older, most of us see our income slowly rise and therefore have a higher standard of living. At the risk of sounding a little glib, wouldn't it be great if we were able to put aside a higher standard of living in order to have a higher standard of giving?

How can we fight back?

These are just three of the ways that the love of money can become a root of evil. How can we fight? Back in 1 Timothy 6, the Lord's answer is clear:

Command those who are rich in this present world ... to put their hope in God, who richly provides us with everything for our enjoyment. Command them to do good, to be rich in good deeds, and to be generous and willing to share. In this way they will lay up treasure for themselves as a firm foundation for the coming age, so that they may take hold of the life that is truly life.   **1 Timothy 6 v 17-19**

Two quick practical applications from these commands:

i. Be rich in good deeds

We have a few men at our church who are deemed rich in this present world. They tend to work very long hours and have little time for much else other than work and their families. They are tired men. The Lord commands them to be rich in good deeds.

Now, this sounds like an added burden, but I think the testimony of guys in this category is that actually it helps. Making the time to mentor a younger Christian in their profession; or making sure that they can lead Bible studies sometimes; or making time to practically serve the church family really helps. These "good deeds" help because otherwise it is easy to become absorbed in money making. Being rich in good deeds is refreshing and helps to prevent them from becoming exhausted by money making.

ii. Be rich in generosity

We are only stewards of the money that God has given us. There is no problem with having a million pounds in the bank, as long as we recognise that it is God's money.

Selfish accumulation is sinful. Wise stewardship to serve Christ is godly. Jesus is famously clear that:

No one can serve two masters ... You cannot serve both God
and money.   **Matthew 6 v 24**

Being generous is a concrete sign of loving God, which
encourages us and others as they see it. Practically, this will
involve sacrifice. It's striking that in Philippians 4 v 18, Paul
describes the giving of the Philippian church as a fragrant
offering and acceptable sacrifice. That is the same expression
used of Christ on the cross. It's extraordinary that God would
use the same expression of our sacrificial financial giving as
he would of Jesus' sacrificial life giving.

If you cannot point to things that you have gone without
in order to be generous to gospel work and others, then that
is troubling. By contrast, to know that you have shopped
more cheaply for food, taken a less expensive holiday, or
cancelled a pleasant subscription in order to give money
away is very personally encouraging. You are not obliged to
do these things, but it is a mark of God's work in us.

The encouragement of 1 Timothy 6 is that, as we are rich
in good deeds and generosity, then we lay up treasure for the
coming age; we... "take hold of the life that is truly life". We
want to invest our money in a way that lasts.

So, *invest in the bank of Jesus Christ*. There is no tax; no
risk. Exponential returns are guaranteed. Follow Christ. Trust
Christ. Bank with Christ. Invest in Christ. You cannot lose.

I have stuck on my wall some wonderful words from the
Puritan preacher, Richard Sibbes:

*Christ himself is ours. In the dividing of all things, some men have
wealth, honours, friends and greatness, but not Christ ... but a
Christian has Christ himself ... Therefore what if he wants those
lesser things, he has the main ... the spring, the ocean in whom all
things are.*

Bible study

Read 1Timothy 6 v 6-10; 17-19.

- Take time to give thanks to God for some of the things that He has richly provided for your enjoyment.

- *People say: "This is the life!"*
  How would you answer them from these verses?

- *Do you think of money as "mine" or as lent to you by God in order to steward? Do you put more thought and planning into your "pension plan" or your "Treaure-in-heaven-Trust with the Lord"?*

- *What helps you to be generous?*

Discuss

- John is a 40-year-old man with a wife and two children. He and his wife became Christians a year ago, and he started tithing his income because he had heard that's what Christians were meant to do. However, he has been giving the issue of money more thought. He turns up at church one day and tells you his intention to give away every penny of his savings to a mission agency. His logic is that he earns a salary which covers the mortgage and most regular outgoings and that from now on he is going to trust God rather than money in the bank. *What would your advice be to him?*

- Darren works at a local supermarket, and is struggling to raise his two children on the wage he takes home. He comes to your home group, and often makes pointed remarks about the quality of the furniture, the size of the house and your car. "It's all right for some!" he is often heard saying. *What should you say to him?*

Phil: *"Feeling the pressure..."*

Spiritually, I think you need to be strong to handle even a modest amount of wealth. Unless you've inherited money, then you are likely to be spending a lot of your time in business or similar circles and the conversations often revolve around housing, private schools and holidays.

I work in this rarefied atmosphere of people who seem numb to any sense of living in the real world, yet they are often persuasive and charismatic personalities.

The danger, and Satan certainly works through this, is that you begin to think that not quite going to the excesses of the people you spend most of your day with actually equates to godliness.

So if they have a Porsche or a Rolls Royce, your new Mercedes or BMW can seem reasonable and humble.

You don't want your children to miss out, so they need to travel for sun or snow during the school breaks, and be indulged about having the latest labels on the clothes they wear.

The result is that the pressure to keep up builds—longer hours in the office rather than at homegroup or the prayer meeting. The kids have slept over at a friend's on Saturday and need picking up on Sunday morning, so realistically church was never on.

I don't think there is such a thing as life balance (at least, I can't find it in the Bible), but you hang onto the idea—rushing from one thing to the next. Anyway, you think: "Surely it's balanced if my wife goes to church and I don't!"

Over time, of course, you begin to believe in your own success, your ability to make money, to look after your family without any need to rely on God. It's a small step to finding yourself irritated by people at church who are struggling in their mundane jobs, and that's exactly where the devil wants us.

In C.S. Lewis's book, *The Screwtape Letters,* the trainee devil is encouraged to get his target to despise the people in his own church family, whose lives he can influence for the better, and instead love Christians in remote unreachable places.

So sending money to missionaries in far-away places while withdrawing from the local church is exactly what the devil wants and, in my experience, it suits the flesh too.

Dave: *"A snare I am happy not to be in..."*

I've been a working man all my life. I've worked on the railways, at a sports centre, in gardening and now in a warehouse. There has not been much money in my family—sadly most of it has been squandered through alcohol abuse.

Where I grew up, I wasn't really aware of the huge gap there is between rich and poor. But since moving to a big city I started noticing the size of the houses. I saw wealth I had never really seen before, and I started to be jealous, and covet what other people had. I was working in an expensive suburb, tending the gardens in huge houses, and I thought: *"I'd love to live here"*.

Comfort and guidance come from reading the Bible daily. It shows me what is really important: sharing everything we have—money, possessions and time. Not pursuing selfish ends. It opened my eyes to see rich, and poor people in a new way.

I see a lot of wealthy people struggling with money. I see them struggling to keep their jobs and their huge mortgages. More than that, I understand that those things are not what brings you real happiness in life. I've met people who have fantastic things who are incredibly sad and lonely. They bring no real certainty to life.

And if you have a lot, you also have a long way to fall. If the Lord decides you're not going to live like that any more, then it can be really hard for you. The Bible says that wealth and prosperity come from the Lord, but then so does calamity!

I believe the less you own, the fewer problems you have. The more you own, the more problems you have—the more complicated your life is. I'm thankful that I don't own a house or a car. Life is much simpler, so I can be more content. I don't have that burden to meet those demands.

We all make choices and have to deal with the consequences. The danger with owning things is that they can become all-consuming. They can become a snare, and that's a trap I'm happy not to be in.

Further help

Craig Blomberg's book *Neither poverty nor riches* is brilliant. His summary conclusions are:

- **Wealth is an inherent good** and Christians should try to gain it.
- **Wealth is seductive,** so giving some of our surplus away is essential.
- **Stewardship is a sign of being saved**; Christians will want to give.
- **Some extremes of wealth are intolerable**; we should work for change.
- **Salvation is the ultimate good God wants**, so we should give to organisations which have that as part of their aim.

Other books worth looking at:
Whose money is it anyway? John MacArthur (Nelson).
Beyond greed, Brian Rosner (Matthias Media).
Cash values, Tony Payne (Matthias Media).

Why does my mouth keep getting me into trouble?

Mike McKinley

Have you ever seen a charge of dynamite explode? It's terrifying to see so much power being unleashed all at once: rocks fly, dirt shoots up into the air in waves, buildings collapse, mountains give way. There's something about that kind of raw power that is captivating.

Well, spoken words are a bit like dynamite. When used well, our speech has tremendous power to honour God, bless others, and accomplish good. When used poorly, words are like a lit match dropped in a dry forest; they can start a blaze that will consume everything around.

Small but powerful

Think of how important spoken words have been in your life. Words that were spoken to you as a child have the power to set you on a course for the rest of your life. If you were told good things about yourself—that you were smart, or good looking, or good at sports—then you probably grew up believing those things and acted with confidence.

But if you were told negative things about yourself—that

you are stupid, or worthless, or ugly—you may still not have recovered from the damage those words did to you deep down.

Words, and how we speak them, are the way that we come to know other people and make ourselves known to them. Words are the way we communicate the things that we love, the things that we find important, what makes us laugh, what has happened to us in the past, what we hope or fear will happen to us in the future. Words are the way we express and communicate ourselves, for good or ill.

Human beings need to communicate. There's something deep down in us that needs to hear other people, to know them and be known by them. We need to be understood, to make ourselves known. And because words are so powerful and so important to our daily existence, the Bible spends a lot time talking about our words.

Two speakers, one choice

Words aren't something that human beings thought up. One of the very first things we learn about God in the Bible is that **he is a God who speaks.** He created the world by speaking it into existence ("Let there be light!"). In Genesis 1 v 26 we see a conversation between the three persons of the Trinity as God says: "Let us make man in our image, after our likeness." And in Genesis 2 v 16-17 God speaks in order to give Adam some instructions for how he and Eve should live in the newly created world.

But God isn't the only one in the universe who speaks. We see in Genesis 3 that the serpent, the devil, also has the capacity to speak. He comes to Adam and Eve and speaks to them, but he has a different message. Satan tells them that his words are the path to true happiness, that they should believe him and listen to his words. Tragically, our first parents listened to the wrong voice.

In a very real way, all of human history from that point to this very moment has been a war of words. On one hand you have God's words, calling us to follow Him and know life and blessing. On the other hand, the speech of the evil one, words intended to enslave and destroy. And every word you speak as a Christian is a salvo in that battle. It either fulfils your calling to live in the image of God, or it displays the image of Satan. Your words will do God's work, or Satan's.

Godly words

So what does it look like to reflect the image of God with your speech? The book of Proverbs gives us a lot of instruction about our speech, and its advice breaks down into three broad categories:

First, godly people speak true words. Proverbs 12 v 22 tells us:

> Lying lips are an abomination to the Lord, but those who act faithfully are his delight."

When we speak the truth, we honour God. We declare ourselves to be on God's side. We are reflecting His image. In Hebrews 6 v 18 we are told: "It is impossible for God to lie." That's not because God is somehow limited in His power and can't figure out how to lie, but rather because it is *always* His desire to be truthful. Speaking the truth is part of what it means to reflect the image of God to the world.

Truthful speech is also a way of taking sides against the devil. In John 8 v 44 Jesus said of Satan:

> "When he lies, he speaks his native language, for he is a liar and the father of lies."

And so the truthfulness of your words will show something of what it is that rules your heart. If you live in the fear of the Lord who does not lie, you will speak the truth.

Second, godly people speak *appropriate* words. Have you ever been in a situation where someone said just the right thing to you? Maybe you were discouraged and someone blew fresh wind into your sails with their words. Or perhaps you were out of line and a friend challenged you on it in a way you could hear without being defensive. There's wisdom in knowing just the right thing to say at a given moment. Proverbs 25 v 11 tells us that: "A word fitly spoken is like apples of gold in settings of silver."

Take a minute to examine your words. Examine the effects that they have on people. Proverbs 15 v 4 tells us: "A gentle tongue is a tree of life, but perverseness in it breaks the spirit." And Proverbs 12 v 18 says: "There is one whose rash words are like sword thrusts, but the tongue of the wise brings healing." God's words were meant to help and strengthen Adam and Eve. Satan's words were intended to destabilize and destroy them.

So ask yourself: do people leave your presence built up and encouraged? Are your words a tree of life? Are they a source of health and refreshment? Or do people leave your presence frustrated, hurt or exasperated with you? Are your words proud, angry, or selfish? Are your words fitting?

Third, godly people speak restrained words. In Proverbs 15 v 28, we are told that "The heart of the righteous weighs its answers, but the mouth of the wicked gushes evil." And Proverbs 17 v 27 says: "Whoever restrains his words has knowledge, and he who has a cool spirit is a man of understanding."

If you are going to have true and appropriate speech,

you are going to have to be thoughtful. It won't happen immediately and naturally. Instead, godly speech requires us to ponder our words before we speak them, because—let's be honest—unless you're really, really godly, the first thing that pops into your head most of the time will be something you probably shouldn't say.

Think about it: your buddy tells you that he's dating your ex-girlfriend, or the bank makes a mistake and charges you a series of outrageous overdraft fees, or your kid draws all over your new couch. If you just give vent to the first impulse that enters your mind in those situations, your speech isn't going to be very godly. So you need to *not* say those foolish words. You need to hold them back, restrain them, listen, and ponder. This is what James 1 v 19 tells us to do: "Let every person be quick to hear, **slow to speak,** slow to anger."

The heart of the matter

My guess is that I don't have to work very hard to convince you that your speech doesn't meet those standards. Imagine if every word you spoke this week were put into a transcript and distributed to your friends, neighbours, family, and co-workers. What picture of you would emerge?

While some of your words may well have been true, appropriate, and restrained, my guess is that you'd have plenty to be ashamed of. Gossip, impatience, anger, anxiety, perversion, jealousy, and cruelty: all of those sins are recurring characteristics in our speech.

Why is that the case? Why do we have such a problem with our words? In one of his most famous sermons, Jesus taught us the source of our word problems:

> For no good tree bears bad fruit, nor again does a bad tree bear good fruit, for each tree is known by its own fruit. For figs are not gathered from thornbushes, nor are grapes picked from

a bramble bush. The good person out of the good treasure of his heart produces good, and the evil person out of his evil treasure produces evil, for out of the abundance of the heart his mouth speaks.

Luke 6 v 43-45

The words we speak are the fruit of our hearts. And so your *word* problems are really a *heart* problem. Your speech doesn't come from nowhere. It springs naturally from your heart; it shows everyone what you are really like.

- **Your anxious words** reveal that your heart doubts that God can be trusted.
- **Your proud words** show that your heart believes that you are worthy of honour and glory.
- **Your angry words** reveal that your heart thinks that you alone must be obeyed and coddled by the universe.

So far this is all bad news. Our sinful words show that we have a sinful heart. But you realise that there is a kind of bad news that really turns out to be good news, right?

Think about it: if you have pain in your chest and you go to the doctor, there is a kind of bad news that is good news. If the doctor tells you that you have a blocked artery, that's bad news. But if the doctor tells you that they have caught it in time, and that there is a solution to the problem that would otherwise kill you—that the blockage can be cleared and your health can be restored—then the bad diagnosis is actually great news for you.

In the same way, our inability to control our speech can be good news. It serves as a diagnostic. It shows us the state of our hearts: proud, angry, and in rebellion against God. And that realisation makes us long for a cure, a cure that God has provided for us in Christ. Jesus, the eternal Word of God, came to save us from our sinful hearts. He lived a life of perfect obedience to God, speaking only gracious and righteous words. But on the cross he took the punishment for our rebellion.

That's the solution to our sinful words. When we come to Christ in faith, we receive a new heart and the gift of God's Spirit. In the life, death, and resurrection of our Saviour we are saved from a wasted life using words to glorify ourselves. We are free from having to clutch and grasp with our words to establish our own glory. Instead, our tongues have been healed and set free to do that for which they were created: *to give God glory!*

Discuss

- *What "sins of the tongue" do you particularly struggle with?*

- *What do your words reveal about the state of your heart?*

- *How can looking to Jesus' life, death, and resurrection help you to make your speech more truthful, appropriate, and restrained?*

Bible study

How do words play a role in the following Bible passages? What does that tell us about God's plan to save and redeem us from our rebellion against him?

- **Genesis 11 v 1-9**

- **Acts 2 v 1-11**

- **Revelation 5 v 11-14**

Further help

Respectable sins, Jerry Bridges (NavPress).

How much screen time is too much?

Wes McNabb

I am writing this on a train. Across the aisle, a man is watching a film on his laptop. He has his headphones on. And while I can't hear it, I can see it.

It's a thriller based in Venice and it looks cool and exciting. I am distracted immediately because the visual impact of the screen is compelling. But as I force my eyes back to my own screen, I look over again and see that a bedroom scene is about to begin. It's hard to look away.

I'm reminded that there are both great and dangerous aspects of TV and computers. They can be fantastic tools for relaxation, communication, laughter and banter with friends and family. They keeps us informed, educated, and in touch with the culture we are part of and seek to reach.

But while it's important to understand the benefits that come from the glare of screens, it's essential we clearly grasp the potential spiritual health hazards associated with them.

The devil's tube?

Our enemy, the devil, has been using TV ever since it was invented. He was also quick on the uptake with computers and the internet. He, being a vicious but very clever adversary, will use anything and everything to harm us. For the devil we are especially easy targets when we are tired and our guard is down. For the Christian man there are two huge areas of danger concerning "screen time"—time and content.

Time

The average person in the UK watches three hours of TV each day—more in North America. So beware even if you watch 50% or 25% of that—it's still a huge chunk of your spare time. Proverbs 4 v 23 warns us: "Above all else, guard your heart". When TV has the priority in my life, my time to do other things is limited. Good, helpful and wholesome things are squeezed out.

To "guard your heart" means guarding your time. Wasting it on TV or computer games robs us of things such as meaningful relationships being established, hobbies and skills being developed and enjoyed, time in God's word and with His people, and reaching others for Christ. Just to name a few.

I know that when I watch too much TV it often makes me physically and spiritually lethargic. I become frustrated that I have wasted so much time that could have been better used in a hundred and one other ways.

When my schedule and church patterns are dominated by what's on TV, I really have got problems that need addressing.

Content

Whether it's bad language, sex or violent content, your TV and computer provide many possible ways of harming the Christian man spiritually.

God's values are rarely at the heart of most programmes and films, so watching requires extreme discernment.

The apostle Paul at the beginning of Ephesians 5 exhorts us, as Christian men, to "be imitators of God ... and to live a life of love". The passage goes on to speak about sexual purity and the avoidance of all obscenity. So we need to understand that what we watch *will* have an influence on us.

For example, when it comes to sex, the TV blatantly lies, giving the impression that outside of marriage, sex is always wonderful and fulfilling. Or that violent revenge is a solution to injustice. There are endless computer games that will allow us to "live out" these fantasies. As men, we are so visually stirred and wired, and images of a violent and sexual nature can stay in our memory banks for years, undermining the truth of God's word.

Millions are spent on TV advertising. Why? **Because it works!** TV does have a massive impact on us.

When too much time and bad content combine, TV can also bring about a desensitising of our consciences. Warnings about things forbidden and harmful are ignored, or not seen for what they are. Our hearts become numbed and hardened to sin, and become dull to the precious things of our holy God.

So what's to be done?
Plenty.

Throw your TV and laptop out? Perhaps for a minority that may be the only option if you can't exercise wisdom and restraint. But that's extreme and, for most, some basic actions will greatly help. That involves being assertive and intentional with your screen habits.

Here are a few suggestions that may be helpful for you:
- **Block channels and websites.** Yes, not just the blatant dodgy ones, but all the ones that show explicit material. That will include some channels that are fine in the day, but take on a vile form in the evenings. Block them for you, not just the kids! Get someone else to put in the password if necessary.
- **Accountability.** Get a good friend who will hold you

to account over what you watch and the websites you visit. Be brutally honest with one another. For married guys your wife will usually be a great help here.

- **No TV in the bedroom.** The worst programmes are on late at night. Bed is for sleeping and other things much better than TV if you are married!
- **Keep a time check.** Add up the screen time you spend over a couple of weeks and share that with godly friends. Then discuss what's reasonable and honourable in God's eyes.
- **Learn verses.** Such as Philippians 4 v 8: "Whatever is true, whatever is noble, whatever is right, whatever is pure, whatever is lovely, whatever is admirable, if anything is excellent or praiseworthy, think about such things". A minister friend of mine says all Christians should write that out on a card and put it on top of their screens!
- **Have a TV and computer fast.** Give yourself a break from screens one day a week now and then just to prove to yourself you can survive without it.
- **Plan what you watch.** When we go to the cinema, it's always to watch something we have researched. Do the same with TV. Don't just watch for the sake of it.
- **Find positive replacements.** There are many great things you can do instead. Don't just *not* watch TV and twiddle your thumbs. Replace it with a whole host of great things: more time with friends and family; pursue or pick up that forgotten hobby that you once loved; go and do something physical rather than adding to the nation's obesity problem by vegetating in front of the box; get a great Christian book out; listen to some amazing sermons online.

When I was a kid growing up, there was a programme called *Why don't you?* It was all about switching off your

TV and getting out and about to do something "less boring instead".

Well, why don't you watch less and be more selective with what you watch for the good of your soul?

They say most of the new channels have not improved TV one bit. But I came across this on a certain Channel 23:

The TV is my shepherd, my spiritual life shall want.
It makes me lie down and do nothing for the cause of Christ.
It demands my spare time.
It restores my desire for the things of the world.
It keeps me from studying the truth of God's word.
It leads me in the paths of failure to attend a place of worship.
Yes though I live to be a hundred, I will still pay the rental.
My telly is with me, it prepares a programme for me,
*   even in the presence of visitors when its volume shall be full.*
Surely comedy and commercials shall follow me all the days of my
life—and I will dwell in spiritual poverty for ever!

Some of you are going to be in a more difficult situation than most, alone or on work trips in a hotel, surrounded by non-Christians in the flat you live in, etc. You will really need to put in extra safeguards to protect yourselves.

Imagine if all of us as Christian men could plan to spend one or two fewer hours a week of wasteful screentime, and instead invested that time in our family and friends, in God's word or in our local church. What a great blessing and joy to our own souls, our communities and churches that would be.

Discuss

- *Honestly, how much casual screen time do you have a week? Are you happy with that?*

- *How do you decide what you're going to watch?*

- *What good reasons do you have for watching TV?*

- *Would your life be considerably better or worse if you did less screen time?*

- *What else could you do with your time if you were to limit the amount you watch? List at least three things you find you "don't have time for" that might become possible with a little more self-discipline.*

Bible study

Look at Philippians 4 v 8-9

1. *What does Paul want us to think about?*

2. *Think about your favourite TV programme for a moment; in what ways is it:*
   - *true?*
   - *noble?*
   - *right?*
   - *pure?*
   - *lovely?*
   - *admirable?*
   - *excellent?*
   - *praiseworthy?*

3. *It may not have many of these things, but that doesn't necessarily mean that we shouldn't watch it. So what benefit is there to be found in watching it? How does it help you:*
   - *in your Christian life?*
   - *understand the damage caused by sin?*
   - *relate to your non-Christian friends?*
   - *appreciate creativity?*

Tom: *"I needed to escape..."*

Computer gaming began as a hobby when I was a teenager. There was nothing really wrong with it; it was just a fun way to spend some time with my Christian friends. Then it became most weekends; then a couple of week nights as well.

It was appealing. It was great fun; exciting and stimulating with a little bit of escapism too. And I could justify all that: I was enjoying God's good creation, spending time with my fellow brothers and having some much needed downtime.

There was never a moment when I decided this was more important to me than my relationship with God. (Although I reacted angrily when that was suggested to me once.) But my actions certainly began to suggest that, then betray that, then shout that I was in danger.

I had stopped reading the Bible and praying on my own, stopped meeting with other Christian guys, and—what scares me most now—my affections were gradually being replaced and I began to become cold to Jesus and other Christian things.

But God is faithful. He had given me one faithful friend

who was concerned enough to push me on the issue. I used to avoid him because he would challenge me about how I was spending my time, energy and money. So I really did know I was being stupid and damaging myself spiritually but wasn't prepared to admit it.

The real breakthrough only came because of a move out of the environment I was in. Removing myself physically from those places, people and patterns which caused me to stumble was the radical impetus I needed and a great mercy. I am very, very thankful to God for this, drastic though it felt at the time.

I still feel slightly vulnerable and often find myself enjoying fond memories of the time I spent, though now I see clearly that it was actually time wasted. I'll not get those years back. I could, and should, have been actively involved in gospel ministry; instead I just frittered them away in front of a screen.

If this sounds like something you're caught in; stop deceiving yourself. "If your right eye causes you to sin, gouge it out." (Matthew 5 v 29)

If not, make sure you are the sort of guy who cares enough to challenge your brothers when you see them sliding; because they probably won't realise themselves until it's too late.

"As iron sharpens iron, so one man sharpens another."

Proverbs 27 v 17

Dave: *The Sopranos and me*

This is a very short story about when we get too into something at the expense of that which nourishes us. This is the tale of when I decided to re-watch *The Sopranos* last year—having initially watched it and loved it as a much younger chap. I got the complete boxed set of all six seasons, and started to dive in.

I watched it when I got home from work before my wife returned (she's not a fan). I watched it while she cooked dinner. I watched it when she popped out to the gym. I was even known to watch it early in the morning, before work and at the expense of a proper quiet time. As Season 1 became Season 2 became Season 3, the characters, events and mood of the programme crept into my dreams, my conversation and my idle thoughts.

Then, sitting in church one day, I came to suspect I had been a bit of an idiot. Jesus had been pushed out of my mind by Tony. Thereafter, with a momentary sigh, I stopped. I haven't watched it since. That's not any kind of binding rule, but it's best for me for the foreseeable future.

And that's it really. This is not about whether you should ever watch *The Sopranos*. This is about the fact that if you want God's word on your mind and on your lips, then you need to give a decent chunk of time to looking at God's word, alongside things that consider and reflect it. If you spend that chunk of time exclusively watching gangsters do their worst... well, your mind and your mouth will probably use a whole different set of words instead.

A prayer

Thank You Heavenly Father for the gift of technology.

Thank You for the way I can relax and enjoy stories and drama brought to life on the screen.

Thank You for the gift of computers, and the way they can make life easier and information more accessible

Please help me to enjoy these gifts in ways that bring honour and glory to You.

Help me to look only at things which are good, noble and true.

And help me to encourage others who have been caught up in the addictions of pornography and gaming.

And help me to grow in holiness, and devote my time to things which please and honour You,

through Your precious Son, my Saviour Jesus Christ.

Amen.

Further help

Captured by a better vision, Tim Chester, (IVP).

Help! He's struggling with pornography, Brian Croft, (Day One)

Why am I so bad tempered when things don't go my way?

Trevor Archer

The grumpy old man has become a stock character in TV sitcoms. And these characters appear on our screens for a good reason. Because they are all around us—we meet them in everyday life!

Why is it that grumbling and bad temper seems to be a particular problem for men, especially as they grow older?

Lots of reasons—but the bottom line is often that life has not turned out as we hoped or thought it would. Success or recognition passes us by; promotion goes to others; tragedy shatters our dreams; relationships turn sour and disintegrate. Disillusioned with life, it's a very small step to cynicism.

"Grumpy" becomes the way we begin to do life. Before we know it, we find it so much easier to spot what's wrong with other people or situations than to see what's right about them. The glass is decidedly half-empty!

Sadly Christians aren't exempt. How many older Christian men do you know who have something of a sour, cynical and snide attitude to life? Answer: *Far too many!* Fact is, grumpy soon becomes a habit, and a very dangerous one!

Grumbling as an art form

The Israelites, who were part of the great escape from Egypt, turned grumbling into an art form. They had been caught up in the great drama of God rescuing His people from Egypt. They had seen first-hand His miracles, signs and wonders. But when the going got tough on the journey to the promised land, these same people soon turned against God and His servant, Moses.

The way in which, in a matter of days, they turned from glorifying God to grumbling against God's servant Moses is almost unbelievable (see Exodus 15). Until, that is, we think how easily we can do the very same thing!

What happened next is a dire warning to Christians. It shows us how utterly seriously God views this matter. He was so angry with their persistent whining that in the end He determined that *none of them* would ever see the Promised Land.

That's because their grumbling betrayed an unbelieving heart—an attitude that says to the Lord:

> *"You've got this wrong. Life is not working out the way I think it should. You've really let me down… You can't be trusted!"*

At the core of grumpiness is the sin of unbelief. It's the mistrust of God's goodness, and resentment at the route He has taken us in life.

So what's the answer?

What's the cure for grumpiness? In a word: *Thankfulness!*

There's a huge emphasis on joyful thankfulness in the New Testament. For example, when Paul writes to the church at Colossae and thinks about their lives, he doesn't lay on them a list of "do's and don'ts". Rather he sets out one simple principle: *Thankfulness!*

> Whatever you do *[sublime or mundane; grimy task or favourite job; at work or at play]* whether in word or deed, do it all in the name of the Lord Jesus, giving thanks to God the Father through him.
> **Colossians 3 v 17**

Thankfulness recognises that **God is in control, not me;** that He is sovereign, not me; that He knows best, not me. Thankfulness trusts God, even when life is hard or it hurts. Thankfulness is a mindset that we are called to nurture and develop in ourselves and in one another.

The Israelites' grumbling and ingratitude was particularly appalling, because they had experienced the rescue of God first-hand from their slavery in Egypt.

But for Christians it is *even more so*. Those who have trusted in Christ have been rescued from judgment and hell; from the clutches of the world, the flesh and the devil. We have been rescued for an eternity of enjoying the immeasurable riches of Christ. How disgraceful that we should allow a grumbling spirit to fester in our hearts. It would be like winning an Olympic gold medal and then complaining about the colour of the ribbon.

Practising thankfulness

In the 18th century, William Cowper lived next door to John Newton in the town of Olney in Buckinghamshire. Together, they were the top songwriting team of their day in the Christian music scene.

Cowper was a celebrated poet, one of the greatest the UK has produced, in fact. But boy, could he do "grumpy"! Poor man, his downbeat demeanour was fuelled by a predisposition to depression and despair, and yet the Lord used it to do something wonderful in Cowper's life and in the lives of thousands who have been helped by his honesty and desire to know Christ.

With Newton's friendship he used the gospel to do battle with his unbelieving, grumpy spirit. In one of his great hymns about prayer he captured the answer to grumbling.

Have we no words? Ah, think again!
Words flow apace when you complain,
And fill your fellow-creature's ear with
the sad tale of all your care.

Was half the breath thus vainly spent,
to heaven in supplication sent,
Our cheerful song would often be –
'Hear what the Lord has done for me!'

So here are a few practical things to avoid becoming a Grumpy Old Man (GOM)—or a young one, come to that!

- Get a grip on grace! Properly understood, grace produces gratitude.
- Remind yourself every day that God is in control. Ask Him for help to trust Him, even when life goes down the drain.
- Get into the habit every day of jotting down or mentally counting off 10 things to thank God for that day. Things He is doing in your life or the lives of others.
- Determine, in the power of the Holy Spirit, not to become a GOM, but rather to grow in grace so you end your days as a GOS – *a Grateful Old Saint!*

Andy: *"Learning to laugh at yourself..."*

I am well known within my family as a grumbler. I come from a long line of complainers, and my father was a notorious curmudgeon (yes, it's in the dictionary), who was known to his grandchildren as "Grumps".

Apart from my genetic predisposition to negativity, the other reason I'm such an enthusiastic complainer is that there is so much in life to complain about. The collapse of the banking system, corruption within the media, cheating in sport, the shallowness of celebrity culture, the indignity of hospital gowns. These are all, the Bible tells us, merely symptoms of the brokenness of life in a fallen world.

However, in my journey as a Christian whinger, I have come to realise that, as John Lennon said in another context, "I am not the only one".

I have been leading a home group in our local church for some years now, and I have observed this to be a problem for many of us as we have grown out of youth into middle age and beyond. So when we meet together, is it our first instinct to find ourselves exercised by the unwillingness of our family and friends to believe the gospel, or the reluctance of our own hearts to live by faith?

Yes, perhaps on our better days, but more often we come burdened by the state of the roads, the poor quality of local services, the mess the government is making of the economy or the way our sports team is being managed.

We recently made a decision to ban moaning and groaning from our meetings, and we are now able to laugh at each other when we lapse into such behaviour, of which, I have come to realise, we are all capable.

We have learned two things together: *first*, to get a

sense of proportion in our experience of the travails of life (none of us has yet received 39 lashes for defending the gospel). *Second*, to pray for each other in the really important issues, for spiritual resilience in the face of abandonment or divorce, or for a real sense of God's presence in the midst of pain and loss.

Discuss

1. *In what particular areas of your life do you struggle with "grumpiness"?*

2. *Do you ever talk openly with another Christian about these struggles?*

3. *What part can other Christians play in helping us avoid being grumblers?*

4. *What would best help you develop a thankful spirit? Be practical!*

Bible study

Read Colossians 3 v 15 – 4 v 2

In this passage there are four specific places where gratitude will be seen in the Christian and the community of God's people.

1. In our relationships (3 v 15)
2. In our meetings together (3 v 16)
3. In the *every* of everyday life (3 v 17)
4. In our prayer life (4 v 2)

Discuss and apply each one

Further help

Respectable sins, Jerry Bridges (NavPress).

Seconds out
ROUND 8

S *tupid. Stupid. Stupid. He felt such a fool for being taken in so easily. As the cornermen got to work on the wicked cut above his eye, he went back over the fight so far...*

Despite his utter terror at the start, the first few rounds had gone surprisingly well. For much of the time, the Adversary had just danced around flinging taunts at him. What punches the Adversary had managed to land were surprisingly soft.

And the guys in his corner had been brilliant. Despite the heckling of the crowd, they had just calmly given him good advice and encouragement. "Keep moving..." "Don't drop your guard..." "Keep watching him and be alert..."

The man had even managed to land a couple of hard ones on his opponent that seemed to rattle him a little. He had staggered back when he had tried a combination, and had gone silent for a couple of rounds. He was beginning to cruise, and started to feel confident... too confident...

It had happened in a flash in the 8th. They were going through the familiar dance, when the brute came at him in a familiar way. Maybe his guard was a little lower than it should have been. Perhaps he was just getting a little too cocky. But this time, instead of a soft blow, easily deflected, he hit him like a pile driver in the stomach.

The wind was blown out of him, and he could offer no defence to the three blows that smashed into his head. Then he was down, the ring whirling around him. He tasted blood and lay in a sea of pain and noise as the count edged towards ten.

How he got to his feet he had no idea. But the training kicked in and he ducked and retreated, staying away from those massive fists that threatened to slam into him.

The bell that signalled the end of the round was a massive relief, as were the willing hands that helped him back to the corner stool. The man sat waiting for the trainer to scream at him, but instead he heard something different.

He leaned forward and urgently whispered in his ear some words that the man could scarcely believe. He looked at him through eyes half closed with swelling.

"It's God's honest truth son," he said. "Now get out there and do your job."

The water that sloshed on his back and face drove away the last traces of dizziness from the pounding he had taken. But it was what the trainer had said that put the heart back in him. He stood up before the bell sounded and stared at his opponent with new resolve for the fight ahead...

Why is it such a struggle to tell others about Christ?

Paul Clarke

L ots of my friends are brilliant evangelists—they love telling people good news. In fact, when they got engaged or married or had their first child or even just when their team won an important match, it was hard to shut them up!

We love sharing good news with other people. So if Christians believe that the message of Jesus is the best news in the whole world, why do we find it so hard to open our mouth and tell others about Him?

Reasons

There are lots of things that stop us. Some of us lack conviction: *How can I talk about Jesus when I have my own doubts?* Some of us lack concern: *Does it really matter if my friends don't believe?* Others lack confidence: *But I'm not sure what to say...* Others still lack courage: *But what if they mock me?* And some lack character: *How can I talk about Jesus when my own life is so inconsistent?*

Whatever the reason, every Christian has a "comfort zone" in evangelism—there is a line that we are not prepared to cross. Here are five real people: **John** has not yet even told his colleagues that he is a Christian. **Simon** is happy to be known as a Christian, but would never speak up for Christ at work. **Jamie** is OK doing street evangelism with strangers, but never talks to his friends about Jesus. **Richard** is happy giving talks to the youth group, but is fearful of inviting his neighbours to church. **Michael** invites people to church all the time, but keeps chickening out of asking his guests to read the Bible with him one-to-one.

The "comfort zone" is a reality for each one of us, but it is rubbish—we need to step out of it. Here are three things to chat and pray about with your Christian friends; may God use them to help us to be just a little bit bolder in talking about Jesus!

1. Remember hell

It's pathetic that, even as grown men, we can be afraid of what other people think of us, but the fear of men is a big barrier to our evangelism. One evangelist put it like this:

We care more about what people think of us now than we care about what God will do to them on judgment day.

The more I think about that sentence, the worse it seems: I care more about the possibility that my friend will not like me if I talk to them about Christ than I care about the certainty that my friend will spend eternity in hell if they do not know Him. That cannot be right.

Love compels us to speak. If we saw a friend swimming in shark-infested waters, we would do everything within our power to get them to safety. If we saw a friend step into the road in front of a bus, we would stop at nothing to get them out of harm's way.

The reality is that people outside of Christ face an even greater danger—they go to hell; if we care about them at all, we will long for them to know the only One who can save them. Jesus Himself said:

> Whoever believes in the Son has eternal life, but whoever
> rejects the Son will not see life, for God's wrath remains on
> him. **John 3 v 36**

The stakes are that high.

2. Remember heaven

Although some of our friends and family have major struggles in life, lots of them are pretty content. Their family life and their career may have a few ups and downs but they are relatively happy with their lot.

As a result, it can feel to us that, if we try and talk to our friends about Jesus, we are inconveniencing them in some way—as though we are hassling them to take out a life insurance policy that they don't really need. But that is to forget just how brilliant the good news of Jesus really is.

When Isaiah looked forward to God's new creation, he compared it to a great banquet:

> On this mountain the Lord Almighty will prepare a feast of
> rich food for all peoples, a banquet of aged wine— the best
> of meats and the finest of wines. On this mountain he will
> destroy the shroud that enfolds all peoples, the sheet that
> covers all nations; he will swallow up death for ever. The
> Sovereign Lord will wipe away the tears from all faces; he will
> remove the disgrace of his people from all the earth. The Lord
> has spoken. **Isaiah 25 v 6-8**

The menu at God's banquet is mouth-watering—"the best of meats and the finest of wines". But even better than the food is the after-dinner entertainment. For God promises that in

His new creation there will be no more crying and no more dying.

It is hard even to imagine how good it will be to live in a world that is free from unemployment and family break-ups and cancer and death. But that is what God offers to us and our friends in Jesus Christ. It is far better than even the best of what this world affords. In his 1949 essay, *The Weight of Glory*, C.S. Lewis famously captured the folly of living for something other than Jesus Christ:

> *We are half-hearted creatures fooling about with drink and sex and ambition when infinite joy is offered to us by God … We are like an ignorant child who wants to go on making mud pies in a slum because he cannot imagine what is meant by the offer of a holiday at the sea. We are far too easily pleased.*

By turning their backs on Jesus Christ, our friends are missing out on so much—in this life and the next. As Christians, we have the enormous privilege of telling people that there is something better than making mud pies in a slum. God has made us the bearers of His generous invitation to a place in His new creation—we get to offer people a place in a glorious eternity!

If we stopped for a minute and thought about just how wonderful the new creation will be, we would not be quite so slow to pass on God's invitation to the people around us.

3. Remember Jesus

Before He ascended to heaven, Jesus told His disciples the job that He wants all Christians and all churches to give ourselves to while we wait for His return:

> Jesus came to them and said, "All authority in heaven and on earth has been given to me. Therefore go and make disciples

of all nations, baptising them in the name of the Father and of the Son and of the Holy Spirit, and teaching them to obey everything I have commanded you. And surely I am with you always, to the very end of the age." **Matthew 28 v 18-20**

There are plenty of people who try to tell us that evangelism is wrong—that it is an act of spiritual imperialism or spiritual racism.

Someone once shouted at me after a talk I gave: "What right have you got to tell me what to believe?" The answer of course is that, in and of ourselves, we have no right to tell people what to believe. But Jesus does. He is the one who has all authority in heaven and on earth. God the Father has already appointed Jesus as Lord of every single human being in the world—all 7 billion of us.

It is a great affront to the glory of Jesus that millions in our country, and billions around the world, continue to commit treason against Him by rejecting His rule over their life. As Christians, we know that Jesus will one day get all of the glory that is rightly His—every knee will bow before Him and every tongue will confess that He is Lord (Philippians 2 v 9-11).

We long for that day, but we long too for Him to be glorified now as sinners turn back to Him in repentance and faith. But how will they turn back to Jesus if they have never heard of Him? And how will they hear of Him unless we tell them?

Every Christian finds evangelism hard and we always will. There is no magic formula that will suddenly make it easy. There are no special techniques that guarantee the results that we long to see. But it is worth persevering anyway because, amazingly, God uses our stumbling efforts in evangelism to save sinners from hell, for heaven and all for the glory of Jesus.

Discuss

- *Lots of things stop us from sharing the good news of the gospel with people. What stops you?*

- *What do you need to be convinced of to overcome that obstacle?*

- *What do you find to be the best bit of the good news?*

Bible study

1 Peter 3 v 14-16

- *How does setting apart Christ as Lord help us overcome our fear and make us ready to speak for Christ?*

- *What is "the hope that we have" and the reason for it? (v 15)*

- *How could you be better prepared to answer people's questions?*

- *What would it look like for us to practise "gentleness" as we give the reason for the hope that we have?*

- *How can we ensure that we show respect in our evangelism?*

- *How can we keep a clear conscience in our relationships with unbelievers?*

Michael: *"I don't want to rock the boat..."*

I struggle to talk about the gospel with my friends for a variety of reasons. I want them to stay my friends, and I don't want them to think I'm an idiot.

Sometimes I just want to relax and be normal with them and around them, and at other times I don't know where to start, so I shy away from saying anything. And some of my friends I see only occasionally so I don't want to rock the boat—I want to catch up with them.

It doesn't help that conversations about the gospel are always messy. They very quickly turn into a conversation about what the Bible says about sex, or whether Christians have happier lives, or some other hot topic.

It's much easier to avoid the topic entirely, and hold out a hope that I can invite them to a gospel talk. Focusing on inviting someone to an event is much easier than actually talking about the gospel.

Two weeks ago I met up with a friend for a drink. We had a good time, and by God's grace, I was able to fight back and put the excuses aside. So what if the world encourages me to care about my standing and reputation, or the flesh tells me to prioritise comfort in good friendships, or the devil tells me I'm not good enough at explaining the gospel?

It's easy to dwell on these things, but for once, I just let them go. The gospel is too important to let those things take over. So I said: "Look. I want the best thing for you. And that's to know that Jesus is Lord of all things." Sure, the conversation didn't stay on track. But we're going to keep talking.

Further help

The gospel and personal evangelism, Mark Dever (Crossway).
How to give away your faith, Paul Little (IVP).
Questioning evangelism, Randy Newman (Kregel).
Bringing the gospel home, Randy Newman (Kregel).
Six steps to talking about Jesus, Simon Roberts & Simon Manchester (Matthias Media).

Why do I still struggle with temptation?

Jason Roach

A couple of years ago, a friend came to me and asked for help in his battle against lust. The first thing I said to him was that I understood. This is a struggle that every man knows.

The apostle Paul said that: "No temptation has seized you except what is common to man" (1 Cor 10 v 13). This means that, although we may have different histories and particular struggles, fundamentally, lust is a struggle we can all relate to.

My abiding memory of that discussion was my friend's courage. It takes courage to put your hand up and admit you have a problem. It takes even more courage to admit that you can't deal with it on your own. When you see courage like that you know that God is already at work.

Much of what follows was learned on the journey we went on as we struggled and prayed together. I hope it might encourage us all to fight the battle against lust courageously too.

We're wired

Part of the reason that we find lust such a struggle is because we are wired for sexual relationships—it's how God made us. So it's not surprising that we yearn for it. And at heart, it's a good thing for a man to look at a woman and enjoy what he is seeing.

But the devil and our sinful hearts take this good desire and warp it into lust. Lust is selfishly to desire sex in a way that breaks the marriage bond—present or future (Matthew 5 v 27-28). Fighting it effectively means remembering some key things about what lust is and who Christ is. In short, lust is *destructive* and *disappointing* but Christ brings *help* and *hope*.

What do we need to remember about lust?

1. It's wrong
The times when I've struggled the most are the times when I've convinced myself that my thoughts and actions aren't actually that bad. We'll never make any progress until we get this straight. But the Bible says that lust is wrong and we are to flee from it (1 Thessalonians 4 v 3-5). That means that being single, having a tired wife, or being stressed are no excuse for mentally undressing women at the bus stop, staring at half-naked celebrities in the newspaper, or turning to internet pornography.

2. It's damaging
Lust and the sexual fantasies that our culture encourages dangerously affect our view of women. We are encouraged to see them as objects we can rank in magazines and web polls, instead of people to be cherished and cared for.

This thinking can also affect future relationships. We end up with all kinds of images and ideas etched in our minds that are hard to shake. Patterns of masturbation established in singleness are not simply "shaken off" when you get married either. All this can be the root of bitter disappointment in relationships and marriage that can take years to undo.

3. It's dangerous

Wrong thinking about women doesn't just affect our view of them, but affects women's views of themselves. It is a tragedy that 1 in 250 women will experience the eating disorder anorexia and 1 in 50 bulimia as teenagers or young adults. The pressure in the culture, of which we can be an unwitting part, is the key factor in all this.

4. It's disappointing

Lust never delivers. It always wants more and is never satisfied. Masturbation and pornography never relieve sexual tension in the long term, but only fuel it, making the desires more intense. You indulge in more explicit thoughts and stimulation, waste more time, find yourself more intensely wracked with guilt, and find that it's harder to praise and serve God.

What do we need to remember about Christ?

The main thing that we need to remember is that Christ is the giver of grace. Here are four key things to meditate on:

1. We're forgiven from sin

Our past sin and failures can weigh us down with guilt. But God says that our sins, even today's sins, are taken as far as the east is from the west (Psalm 103 v 11-12). No matter what we've done, no matter who we've done it with, or how many times we've done it, we are *completely forgiven* if we trust in Jesus (1 Pet 3 v 18). We can let go of our guilt!

2. We're free not to sin

Sometimes it feels as if we could never break out of our cycles of lust, guilt and shame. But Romans 6 v 4 makes it clear that Christians live a resurrection-empowered "new life". We no longer *have* to sin. We do not *have* to give in to lustful thoughts and actions today. Christ, the ultimate spiritual warrior, fights sin for us (Galatians 2 v 20). Yes, we will fail. Yes, there will be setbacks. But Christians have Christ's power at work within them to fight sin.

3. We'll one day be free from sin

Progress in the fight against lust can often be slow. Sometimes we feel as if we take as many steps backward as forward. However, God promises that one day we will be like Jesus (1 John 3 v 2). He will finish the good work he has started in us (Philippians 1 v 6). One day we will be freed from lust completely. God is far more committed to changing us than we are, and He has promised to do it! That can be really encouraging when we feel overwhelmed by failure.

4. We'll be fully satisfied

It's easy to feel as if we're missing out. Everyone else is having sex like mad and we're not. The reality, of course, is often far from this—for single *and* married people. But more importantly, Jesus says we're not going to miss out. Sex in marriage is just a picture of life with Him for eternity (Ephesians 5 v 22-33). Life with Jesus will be a purified, intense pleasure that we can't even comprehend now. Whatever our relationship situation now, we will not feel shortchanged in eternity. All that we are looking for in sex now will be ours in Jesus for ever.

What can we do as we struggle?

Here are some practical tips as we fight to see our sin and our Saviour rightly:

- **Stay connected to the church.** Our local church is the place where week by week we get reminded that Christ provides help and hope. It's encouraging that we are freed from the penalty of sin, the power of sin and one day from the presence of sin. Worshipping God, praying to Him, serving His people and being reminded of His grace are essential tools in the struggle against lust.

- **Develop accountability.** Ephesians 4 explains that maturity in the faith comes as we encourage one another in love in our local church contexts (Ephesians 4 v 14-15). That's exactly what my courageous and godly friend sought out. It will feel really awkward and hard and cringe-worthy, especially at first. But over time we need to develop relationships with one or two we trust, where we can begin to share our struggles in this area.

- **Know your weakpoints.** Tim Chester helpfully says that the times when we are most likely to sin are when we are Hungry, Alone, Lonely or Tired (H.A.L.T.). Knowing our particular weakpoints can help us start the fight earlier with prayer and avoidance tactics. Do something other than turning on the television or computer if you are finding it a particular temptation at a certain time of day. Get something to eat, go for a run, leave your door open or ring a friend when you feel weak.

- **Pray for women.** When you come across women who attract your attention for any reason, why not pray for them? Pray that they would be a sister in heaven. God has a habit of changing us through our prayers. If we pray for people we struggle with, God will help us to cherish them as he does.

- **Focus on your wife.** If you are married, then concentrate on developing your relationship with your wife. Focus on those things about her that you love spiritually and physically. Telling her will be an encouragement to you both! Try to get to a point where you can talk about sex and your struggles in general terms. If you struggle with masturbation, perhaps your wife could be involved with that or aware so that it is not a secretive thing.

Conclusion

The key battle then is to remember that lust is destructive and disappointing but that Christ brings help and hope. When we focus on particular sins like masturbation and make them the sole focus of our struggle, we miss the point. The battle is for the desires of our heart. We must remember that God hates our sin but pours out grace to forgive us and to help us to change. Part of that gracious provision is the church to help and support us along the way. My prayer is that, like my friend, we would be a courageous generation of men who take hold of the grace that Christ offers.

Discuss
What is your answer to these three questions?
- *What is it about lust that we need to remember most?*

- *How have you been encouraged by the grace of Christ?*

- *What one practical step could you take in the ongoing fight against lust?*

Bible study

Read Titus 2 v 11-14

What has God's grace (v 11) provided for us:
- in the past (v14a)?

- in the present (v 14b)?

- for the future (v 13)?

How do these three things help us to keep fighting lust?

A prayer

Loving Heavenly Father, I run to You today with great remorse and great rejoicing.

Thank You that Your grace towards me is far bigger than my sin towards You.

Thank You that Your grace covers my sins past, present and future.

In my struggle against sin, give me genuine sorrow, not just temporary guilt.

Sensitise me again to the horror of my sin, the awfulness of my entrapment, and yet the wonder of Your grace.

Help me to find help and hope at the foot of the cross.

Help me to entrust myself to others who will walk with me on the path of repentance.

In Jesus' name, Amen.

Gavin: *"Sin always leads to regret..."*

I'm a single Christian guy, and thought I had this area of my life under control. To my surprise, I started to develop a new struggle in the area of sexual sin in recent years.

By this I mean what the Bible describes as sensuality, lust, a lack of self control, and at times looking at very unhelpful content online. God has been teaching me the seriousness of my sin, the riches of his grace, and the ongoing spiritual battle at the level of my heart.

I've been reminded that although sexual sin may feel pleasant at the time, it is deceptively warring against my soul to ensnare and enslave me. The easier it becomes to get into a particular bad habit, the harder it gets to escape from it, and sin always leads to regret.

God has disciplined me often through painful and

frustrating circumstances, demonstrating both His fatherly love for me and His abhorrence of my sin. I've seen that sexual sin sometimes *seems* private but *always* has implications, often in how closely I am walking with the Lord and how well I relate to others. I'm also struck by the Bible's imperative for a young man to fight sexual sin and develop self control.

As I've seen the seriousness of my sin more clearly, God's grace is all the more striking. I know that at root my heart is the issue, and so the answer to sexual sin is ultimately drawing near to God and growing in love for Jesus Christ.

In looking to fight better I have found several practical strategies helpful. *First*, it has been good to identify close friends I feel able to share my struggles with. *Second*, it has encouraged me to seek God's presence with me more as I go into the day, to identify times when I am vulnerable, and to avoid spiritually dangerous situations where appropriate. *Third*, it's helpful to remember some key verses. God has been reminding me that, however I feel when tempted, sexual sin is deceptive and serious, and God is always good and provides a way out.

Further help

Sex is not the problem (lust is), Joshua Harris (Multnomah).
Every man's battle, Stephen Arterburn and Fred Stoeker (Water Brook).
Captured by a better vision, Tim Chester (IVP).

Although this chapter is entitled *Girls*, we recognise that some men will struggle with same-sex attraction. If this is you, then the following might be helpful:
What some of you were, Christopher Keane (Matthias Media).
www.truefreedomtrust.co.uk

My life seems so ordinary. Why hasn't God given me more?

Wanyeki Mahiaini

"God must have loved the ordinary events because he made so many of them." Abraham Lincoln

Taking inspiration from the quote above someone has added: "And God must love ordinary people because he made so many of them too."

I am one of them; ordinary height, ordinary weight and although they won't thank me for saying it, my friends are… well… ordinary. The majority of jobs I have done have been ordinary teaching jobs. My wife and I, and our two grown-up children, live in an ordinary house.

It is good news for those of us whose lives seem so ordinary. In the next few pages, I want to offer you a few things to think about the next time you are tempted to think: *"My life seems so ordinary. Why hasn't God given me more?"*

Circumstances

First, ordinary circumstances are a good thing. They give us time to reflect on important things.

"Ordinary" suggests that things are at some form of

equilibrium. For example, when you go to the doctor and the results show nothing unusual—nothing out of the ordinary—it is very good news. What can be true of individuals can also be true of nations. After a period of dreadful upheaval, the nation of Israel under David and Solomon experienced peace when everything seemed quiet and normal.

It was during this period (when nothing out of the ordinary was happening politically or socially) that a lot of the "wisdom material" in the Bible was written. Perhaps the ordinariness of the times gave the writers of the wisdom books time and space to reflect on the meaning of life. It gave us such jewels as *Proverbs*, *Ecclesiastes* and the *Song of Songs*.

Paul urges Timothy to pray for our leaders so that such a state of peaceful "ordinariness" may prevail, and we may "live a quiet life" (1 Timothy 2 v 2).

So rather than *resenting* an ordinary life, perhaps we should instead *thank God* for the absence of any major crisis in our lives, for the regular rhythm of each day, and the opportunity it provides for quiet reflection. How about building a pattern of Bible reading and prayer into our lives? The length of a quiet time is hardly the point. The point is to give ourselves time to slow down, and listen to the voice of God as He makes sense of our existence in the Scriptures.

I do not apologise for making such a predictable suggestion. Wiser men and women than me—both living and "asleep in Christ"—have given the same counsel. My mornings are fairly predictable. If I log onto the web for news before I have a quiet time, you can be sure I have chosen not to have a quiet time that day. So I work at that discipline every morning.

God at work
Second, ordinary people are a very good thing. They remind us that God uses the ordinary to achieve the extraordinary.

The world's way of measuring success is in terms of expertise and charisma. If we strive for success on the world's basis, we will become mere activists. And that can only lead to guilt and failure.

Being skilled in knowledge and having a lively character aren't evil in and of themselves, but they are bad if they become the goal.

If God has given us these things, then we need to beware the pride, arrogance and self-confidence that can so easily result. If God has wisely chosen to give us a more modest measure of these things, then our temptation is to envy others, be bitter towards God and to assume that we are therefore inadequate or second rate in the kingdom of God. Nothing could be further from the truth as Paul makes clear:

> My grace is sufficient for you, for my power is made perfect in weakness. Therefore I will boast all the more gladly about my weaknesses, so that Christ's power may rest on me. That is why, for Christ's sake, I delight in weaknesses, in insults, in hardships, in persecutions, in difficulties. For when I am weak, then I am strong. **2 Corinthians 12 v 9-10**

Growing up in Kenya, I was very attracted to a movement called Liberation Theology, which sanctioned the use of force to bring about justice. Camilo Torres, a young Colombian priest, became a hero of mine for giving up his cassock and taking up a gun "to become more truly a priest". Under his influence I dropped my foreign baptism name and became quite disillusioned with Christianity as I knew it then.

But then, in His wisdom, God made my path cross with a Danish Christian worker. No two people could have been more different. I was a young, passionate third-world rebel, and he was a middle-class, middle-aged guy from the first world. I wanted to change the world through radical economics. He wanted to change me through the Bible!

In spite of our differences, and his inability to enter into my world, he persisted in meeting up with me for Bible study for two years. I frequently did not show up for our meetings, but he always did. Somewhere in that dysfunctional relationship, and the very ordinary act of opening the Bible together, the Bible did its work and I began to grow as a disciple. Today you can cut me any way you want and you will find a deep commitment to personal discipleship centred on Bible study.

God uses ordinary people such as my Danish friend to do extraordinary work. You may feel very ordinary as a Christian, but something as ordinary as opening up the Bible with someone will produce extraordinary results. Such faithfulness is real "success" in the kingdom of God.

Discipleship

Third, ordinary people in ordinary circumstances are the perfect opportunity for discipleship. If we don't do discipleship, the non-Christian world will do it for us.

Consider the following ordinary scene. A young man steps out of the London Underground, and as he rides the escalator towards the exit, he'll receive dozens of explicit and subliminal (read "discipleship") messages in the adverts, telling him what sort of lifestyle is desirable.

As he exits the station, he'll be handed a free newspaper filled with similar adverts, and the opinions of clever, funny, attractive people, eager to influence his thinking. He can throw the newspaper away without any thought to the cost to the environment.

He steps into a famous clothes shop and buys a new pair of shoes. They're a bargain! But he is not encouraged to think about the children labouring in factories which means that he can buy them so cheaply. The unspoken "discipleship" message as he walks out of the shop is: *"Regular shopping is good therapy. Enjoy"*.

All this happens without a "discipler" in sight. But make no mistake, a sophisticated form of discipleship is taking place all the time. If Christians don't do discipleship, the non-Christian world will do it for us.

The Great Commission in Matthew 28 v 18-20 is to make disciples of all nations and to teach them to observe all that Jesus taught us. There is no get-out clause. *All* Christians are under that commission. In fulfilment of that work, our diaries should *all* look different. This begs the question: If the world is that good at making their own disciples, how are Christians to make disciples of Jesus Christ?

I think the answer lies in being involved in *relational discipleship.*

Relational discipleship means entering into other peoples' worlds and walking with them in the mundane and the extraordinary things of life, and using those situations to point them to Christ, the discipler of the church.

And this is exactly what Jesus did with His disciples. In John 1 v 14 we read:

The Word became flesh and made his dwelling among us. We have seen his glory, the glory of the One and Only, who came from the Father, full of grace and truth.

The sense is that Jesus moved into our back garden and set up home there. Or for a student, Jesus moved into our halls of residence and lived with us. We saw Him at breakfast, lunch and dinner. We saw Him at lectures and at His desk. It means His disciples saw Jesus doing ordinary things; using the ordinary to teach them about extraordinary spiritual truths:

- He used the experience of a hot, dry and thirsty afternoon to teach about living water.
- He used a wedding party to teach them that He is the one who brings the wine of the new kingdom.
- He used a storm at sea to teach them to trust Him.
- He used ordinary bread to teach them that He is the bread that will last for ever.
- He took a little child in His arms and taught them about true faith.

In the same way, ordinary Christians can use ordinary events that happen every day to teach each other about the extraordinary:

- A missed appointment can open the door to talk about grace and forgiveness.
- A drink at the pub can present an opportunity to talk about the influence friends have on us.
- A one-to-one Bible study on 2 Timothy 2 v 2 will give us the chance to talk about becoming disciple-making disciples.
- The sight of a beautiful girl can spark a conversation about true beauty, and what to look for in a wife.
- Eating international food can prompt a discussion about the gospel at work in other countries, and our own.

The worst that can happen in one-to-one or triplet discipleship is that you end up with a good friend. The best that can happen is that you end up with a friend and a growing disciple of Jesus Christ.

It is no big deal for almighty God to create a universe out of nothing. That is what God does. But for God to use an ordinary person such as me to grow His church in any way—that is extraordinary. And God is doing this all the time.

In the New Testament He used many ordinary people,

including one called Timothy. This young man seemed to have a weak constitution and a self-effacing nature . But God used him to disciple whole churches. He used Epaphroditus in the Philippian Church, in spite of his suffering and ill health. All over the world God is using ordinary people in amazing ways.

If God has given you wonderful gifts, then be thankful, but use them for His glory—not your own.

If God has wisely chosen to give you a more modest measure of these things, then rejoice that you are in no way side-lined in the purposes of God. Do what you can for the gospel given the ability, capacity and opportunity that God *has* given to you.

Discuss

- *How can you discover your spiritual gifts in order to serve the church? How can you begin to use them?*

- *Who can I approach about doing a one-to-one or being part of a discipleship triplet?*

- *"There is no unemployment in the church, only work-shy people." Discuss!*

Bible study

Read Philippians 2 v 19-30

- *What was it about Timothy that Paul found praiseworthy?*

- *In what ways have I recently shown a genuine interest in the practical and spiritual welfare of others?*

- *What was it about Epaphroditus that Paul found praiseworthy?*

- *In what practical ways can we take care of others' needs?*
  - *In our small group?*
  - *In our family?*
  - *In our workplace?*

Further help
What is vocation, Stephen Nichols (P&R).
Don't waste your life, John Piper (IVP).
*One2One Guides (various) (*The Good Book Company).
One to one, David Helm (Matthias Media).

John: *"The way I thought about my life changed for ever..."*

I'm a young man with just a few qualifications. I'm pretty ordinary really. But I have a condition called Tourette's Syndrome. It can be really challenging at times, but I thank God for it. People think I must be really unfortunate. But God has used it in amazing ways.

But I've not always thought of it like that. When I was younger I used to get really frustrated at the way that God had made me. I was quite a handful. Occasionally my parents used to have to restrain me to protect me from doing something dangerous or damaging.

As a teenager I couldn't be independent like lots of other kids my age. I used to stand out as being different, because I couldn't control or predict what my muscles would do. As I grew older things got better. I got used to it, and began to accept the fact that I had this condition.

I remember reading Romans 8 one day and it's as though I really understood something important at last. Up until that point I thought my Tourette's was a *bad thing*. But I suddenly realised that *it could be a thing God used for good*. I could use it for His glory. At that point, the way I thought about my life changed for ever.

It's actually helped in my relationship with God. He's given me peace and I trust Him. I can believe that He's been good to me because of all He's done for me in Jesus. I know it doesn't seem like it looking at me from the outside, but He has made my life so much fuller and richer.

My condition means it's very difficult to find employment. My speech can make me hard to understand. But I receive some government funding and my parents are very supportive. This means that I don't have to worry about money and that I can now volunteer for organisations. I'm currently helping out at a Christian organisation and I love it.

I think that God has used my condition to help me be sympathetic to others. I think I can show love to those who suffer in some sort of way and who find it tough because I know how they feel.

And although there are lots of things that I'll never be able to do at church, I still want to be servant-hearted. There are lots of jobs that I can do. Some of the more humble ones. And so I can steward and help lift and shift stuff. And I can support what we do by turning up.

I love a drink, but how much is too much?

Tim Thornborough

> *John sat proudly at the table, a glass of sparkling fizz in his hand, as he looked round the rest of the room, enjoying the laughter and animated conversations. To see his daughter married to such a fine Christian man was the fulfilment of all his prayers. He sipped again and enjoyed the gentle buzz in the room. "God is good," he thought...*

Alcohol has been a battleground for believers since the opening pages of the Bible, and it continues to divide opinion today. Should we be teetotal? Should we only have an occasional glass with a meal? Or should we be much more relaxed about the whole thing?

It's hard to get a balanced view because of the very obvious downsides of drinking, and because we are all vulnerable in different ways to its dark side. But the place to start is surely to see that alcohol is a wonderful gift from God.

The Scriptures speak positively about wine as a gift from God that "gladdens the heart" (Psalm 104 v 15). We should enjoy the good things that alcohol does for us—its taste and its mild effects—and for how it helps us enjoy life, the company of others, and the way it can help us relax and celebrate.

Drink should also remind us of our glorious hope and future. In the Bible, wine is used as a picture of the kingdom of God and of the great wedding banquet of the Lamb that all who belong Christ will enjoy. So it should also be a trigger for us to remember that *"the best is yet to come."*

So alcohol should be something that we can and should *delight* in as Christians. Our approval of it should not be grudging in ourselves or others. It can be something we enjoy, guilt-free, from God's hands and give thanks for:

> For everything created by God is good, and nothing is to be rejected if it is received with thanksgiving, for it is made holy by the word of God and prayer.   **1 Timothy 4 v 4**

But while being enthusiastic about enjoying what God has given us, we need to heed the Bible's clear warnings that this wonderful gift has a significant downside in our fallen world. The world, the flesh and the devil each have their hand in turning something that should be *delightful* into something potentially *disastrous*.

Drunkenness

We tend to joke about drunkenness—but it really is no laughing matter. It's all too evident on a Friday and Saturday night on the streets of our cities.

If you have never witnessed what the binge-drinking culture is doing to our young people, then it's worth taking an educational trip to see what it is like when the clubs shut at 3am; it will help you understand the worldly pressures that our young men and women are facing today.

It's glaringly obvious too in the rising trends towards alcohol-related death and illness at a younger and younger age. It is in plain view on our TV screens as "reality" TV lifts the lid on the lives of others. Drunkenness is a disaster.

And the Bible agrees, but for different reasons.

The more we drink, the more we lose control: of our tongues, our speech, our emotions, our clear thinking, our bodies. And that leads to physical and relational harm. We put ourselves in a place where we can wound others by saying hurtful or stupid things, lose our tempers or be unfaithful. But for Christians, it also causes spiritual harm. As we fail to control ourselves, Christ is dishonoured.

The Holy Spirit is at work in our lives to make us more like Jesus. The Spirit is working to grow fruit in our lives that is exactly the opposite of what alcohol does. He wants us to be patient and kind and self-controlled. Drunkenness leads to the opposite. That's why Paul puts them as direct opposites:

And do not get drunk with wine, which leads to debauchery.
Instead be filled with the Spirit.   **Ephesians 5 v 18**

So just to be clear. If you are a Christian you should make it your aim *never* to be drunk. *Ever.*

This is where the world can exert a powerful influence on us. Whether it's drinking with friends while watching football, or enjoying to excess the fine wines at a formal dinner with business colleagues, it's very hard to say "no" when someone invites us to have another. We can feel as if we are breaking friendship with them, judging them, or spoiling their evening.

If you struggle with this, then always arrange to drive to wherever you are going—then you have a ready-made reason to not drink. Or be prepared to say positively: "I'm done for the night thanks". And if they ask, be prepared to tell them that you don't like to get drunk because you're a Christian. But you then need to follow up your refusal by showing them that you can have a great time without sliding under the table at the end.

And remember Paul's words to Timothy. Sometimes it's better simply to flee temptation—just leaving may feel like failure, but it is really a success!

Dependency

But there are other ways that the hard stuff can get its hooks into us. We may not get drunk, but we can get dependent on drink in ways that are unhealthy—both physically and spiritually.

What can start as enjoying a "relaxer" after a long hard day can become a routine, until you discover that you cannot really chill out without a glass in your hand. You may not think of yourself as an alcoholic—you may never actually get drunk—but if you find yourself psychologically dependent on drink, so that you are seeking it out, then that is exactly what you are.

There are good websites that show safe levels of consumption, and some helpful self-assessment tests to check where you are at with this. An idol is a "good thing" that becomes a "god thing". When we become dependent on alcohol, we are making an idol of it, and it inevitably pushes out the Lord as the first love in our hearts. Alcoholism is the end point of that idolatry—when we turn to alcohol to deal with our difficulties, rather than turning to the Lord. It needs to be dealt with.

I plan to go teetotal for *at least* a month every year, just to check how I am doing in this area. If you discover that this is a problem for you, talk to your friends, your family or your minister about how you deal with it before it becomes a bigger problem.

For people who struggle with this issue, the simple act of taking communion can be turned from a blessing into a curse.

If that's you, then don't suffer alone. God has put us in the Christian family for a very good reason—so we don't have to walk alone with the burdens we carry. Talk with a Christian friend about how you can start to get a handle on it.

Distraction

The devil will tell us when we are younger that drinking is a way of showing how *grown up* and *manly* we are. He will tell us when we are older that appreciating fine wines or enjoying malt whisky shows how *mature* and *sophisticated* we are. The world will tell us that we need to "just go along with" what everyone else does in order to have a good time. Our own flesh, at various times, will tell us that we can use booze to forget, or punish ourselves, or find joy when we are down, or find the courage to go wild, or escape from pressure at work or at home.

But we need to counter these arguments by reminding ourselves that we are only truly mature men *in Christ;* that the world's way is the easy broad road that leads to destruction; that *Jesus* is our joy, our strength and our refuge in trouble, not a bottle.

I don't believe that drink is a yes or no question. How we handle drink will differ from man to man. It may change in different circumstances and stages of life. It may differ in different company.

We want to relish God's good gift, and enjoy drink as part of how we enjoy each others' company and conversation. But we don't want to allow it to divert us from our main focus: growing like Christ, and making him known to a lost and dying world. Nor do we want our liberty to become a stumbling block for a brother who is tempted in a different way from us.

So, as I meet up with friends, I'll never get "legless", because I need to be the one with beautiful feet that brings the Good

News to them. I won't become a lackey to liquor, because I want to enjoy the freedom I have in Christ and show everyone how good it is to be dependent on God for life and everything. And I won't get distracted by drink, because I want to set my mind on living for Christ and helping others discover the riches of his grace.

Discuss

- *What is your own experience with alcohol?*

- *If you drink, can you say why you drink?*
  Is that a good reason?

- *If you don't drink, why do you avoid it?*
  Is that a good reason?

- *How would you teach a young man to drink?*
  How would you help him to have good motives in what he does with alcohol?

Bible study

Read over the following warnings and encouragements from the book of Proverbs.
How do you think we should apply each one?
- 23 v 19-21
- 23 v 29-30
- 23 v 31-33
- 23 v 35
- 31 v 4-5

Jonathan: *"I can't keep on living like this..."*

When I committed my life to Christ at college, I knew that getting drunk needed to stop. At the beginning, I did well. I went from being drunk several times a week to not at all. And it was great.

But looking back, I'd been relying on my own efforts to stop. And gradually, as the exciting newness of being a Christian wore off, I began to have one too many, now and then. And 18 months later, I was back to getting drunk pretty much as often as I had done before. I excused it—told myself I hadn't been *that* drunk, or that it didn't really matter. Sometimes I said sorry to the Lord—but looking back, I wasn't really sorry. I had no intention of actually changing.

Getting drunk was what my friends did; it seemed a compulsory part of having a fun life; and I wanted Jesus to be my rescuer while ignoring Him as my ruler. But giving up on Jesus as my Lord in one area pretty soon coloured most of the rest of my life. Looking from the outside, you'd have said I'd given up on Christianity altogether.

Then, two summers after I came to Christ, I heard someone pray and they said, as Paul did in 1 Timothy, that they were the worst sinner of all. And something clicked in my head and I thought: "No, I am the worst. Look at what I'm doing—asking Jesus to die for me and yet hating His rule. I can't keep living like this. It's got to be all or nothing."

Crucially, this time I asked God to help me—to do what I'd failed so dismally to do myself and help me with the drinking. I went alcohol free, and it was brilliant. Not only was I no longer in my miserable sinning-and-then-excusing-or-ignoring-it state; I had much more money, and I got loads of chances to explain why I didn't want to get drunk.

Now, ten years later, I'm OK. I can have a few drinks without having a few too many. But I learned two huge lessons through it: that trying to have Christ as rescuer while living as the world does is tense and miserable; and that I need to rely on the Holy Spirit to do what I can't—change my actions, my thoughts and my desires.

Further help

Listed below are some resources that represent two sides of this discussion. For a typical explanation of an "alcohol-free" approach, read:

* *Should Christians drink?* Peter Masters (Wakeman Press).

For a "permissible in moderation" view, try:

* *God gave wine*, Kenneth Gentry (Oakdown Press).

For a history of the debate on this issue:

* *Drinking with Luther and Calvin* (Oakdown Press).

If you are concerned about addictions, a good place to start is:

* *Addictions: A banquet in the grave: Finding hope in the power of the gospel.* Edward Welch (P&R).

Is it wrong to be passionate about winning?

Richard Perkins

My active participation in sport used to involve actually playing. That's less true now. I let others play sport these days. And now I "just" watch.

But I'd never really thought through the issue of godly sports watching. My wife, however, has—on my behalf. She spotted my insatiable appetite for sport early on and took decisive action. She banned *Sky Sports Channel*. She thinks it'll take over my life ... and hers ... and the family's.

She has a point.

We don't have *Sky* any longer.

But how do we watch, and participate in sport in a way that brings glory to God? It may be something you've never thought about before. But every area of our life must come under the lordship of Jesus. So here are three things to ponder as you reflect on your relationship with whatever beautiful game you are attached to...

1. Don't deny the goodness of God
Sometimes we get so immersed in sport that we forget where it's come from. **It's a good gift of God.** Technically

God didn't create it; people did. But using our God-given imagination, we have invented a dizzying array of competitive activities that can get us shrieking with excitement, or endlessly analysing the tactics, personalities and data. From canoeing to kabbadi, Formula 1 to triathlon, sport expresses our creativity, that has its origins in God. There is truly something beautiful about sport because it can reflect the glory of God.

And God gave sport for our enjoyment. Paul says:

> For everything God created is good, and nothing is to be
> rejected if it is received with thanksgiving, because it is
> consecrated by the word of God and prayer. **1 Tim 4 v 4-5**

Since sport is a gift from God to be enjoyed for what it is, we *can* and *should* thank him for it. So before I sit down to watch *Match of the Day*, I ought to pray and give thanks for what I'm about to receive!

Sport is a good thing, so we shouldn't be afraid of being entertained by the skills of great players, even our opponents. We should love the experience of playing in a team, or of sharpening our solo skills on the tennis court against someone better than us. It's OK to derive great pleasure from being caught up in the thrill of competition, so long as we recognise where the joy of sport has its true source. Our loving heavenly Father.

This is important to understand, because not everything that comes out of sport is wholesome, so we can end up thinking that sport is intrinsically evil.

But it's not.

People are. And that's different.

There's *nothing* inherently wrong with sport. Not even with competition, which sometimes gets a bad press with

Christians. But we do need to remember that there is *bad competition* and *good competition*.

Bad competition is what you get when people compete in the wrong way or for the wrong reasons. Sport played like this can be ugly and negative. But it doesn't have to be that way.

In good competition both teams aim for victory. There's usually a winner and a loser. It's the way of finding out how good a team is. And it's also the opportunity to improve. And the best sporting experiences usually take place when two evenly matched teams or individuals go head to head.

But whether I'm watching Barcelona against Real Madrid with a purist's eye for the beauty of the game or whether I'm watching Djokovic and Nadal slug it out in a fiercely contested Wimbledon final, I can still thank God for giving me sport.

Let's not be ungrateful for one of God's good gifts.

2. Don't exaggerate the amount of attachment

Sport works because we belong to a team. We become part of that team and they become part of us. We're attached. They represent us. And we identify with them.

Usually there's a good reason for that. Maybe you support your football team because you were born and raised near the stadium. Perhaps your family has a long-standing attachment to the team that made going to matches with your father and grandfather a strong bonding experience (when you could afford it!).

The stronger our attachment to the team is, the greater our sense of identification. Our fortunes are intertwined. Our moods ebb and flow on the back of their performances and results. I still have to battle not to descend into the pit of despair after another lamentable England performance on the rugby field. There's nothing much wrong with that. It's good to be part of something bigger than ourselves.

But let's just step back for a moment. We have many things we identify with—our family, our birthplace, our profession, our country, our sports team. But the gospel reminds us that **the most important and foundational identity we have is with Christ.** He is who we're about first and foremost. All my other loyalties, even to family, must come second to Him. So *I must never attach myself to a team in such a way that I forget or compromise my true identity in Christ.*

I might be a passionate supporter of my football team, but I'll never be sold out to them in the way some of the die-hard fans are. Not primarily. And it's because I'm a Christian. That's who I am more than anything else. I belong to Jesus Christ. And He belongs to me. That's got to change how I think about my team. And their performances. I can complain about how badly England have played. But it's not the most important thing in the world. It's not even close.

It'll mean, strangely, that sometimes I'll have more in common with one of my team's opposing players or supporters who is my brother in Christ, than I do with my own. It will mean that I will not blind myself to sin and injustice when my team is clearly in the wrong.

I once played rugby against the evangelist, Rico Tice. It was a hard-fought match which had some uncompromising tackles in it. But because we knew each other a little it was fantastic catching up with him in the bar afterwards. I had so much more in common with him than my own team mates. And it showed. Playing sport, or watching sport with Christian friends, can be really wholesome because we can remind one another not to get too caught up in identifying with our team.

So let's not overstate the level of connection we have with

our sporting heroes. There's a connection but it's nothing like what we have through faith in Christ. Paul said:

> I have been crucified with Christ and I no longer live, but Christ lives in me. The life I live in the body, I live by faith in the Son of God, who loved me and gave himself for me.
>
> **Galatians 2 v 20**

Now that's an attachment to get really excited about!

3. Don't ignore the dangers of idolatry

Playing or watching sport can be an "immersion experience". Crucial and exciting games get under our skin and into our hearts so that we love it. That should start to ring warning bells for any believer.

The problem is we can love it too much. It can become our obsession. We can take a "good thing" and turn it into a "god thing". We can end up worshipping it and living for it. It becomes a substitute spiritual life by providing us with sporting heaven or sporting hell.

When the sporting gods smile on us, we're lifted to states of ecstatic praise so that we're indescribably happy. And when they don't, we descend into a pit of morose despair so that we're unbearably miserable.

Do you recognise that picture in yourself? I know whether I'm losing the fight against idolatry if I ask myself a couple of simple questions.

We usually *think* about the things that we most value. So I ask myself:

Richard, where does your mind go when you have nothing else to think about?

We usually *talk* about the things that we most value. So I ask myself:

Richard, what's the subject of your most passionate conversations?

We usually *find time* for the things that we most value. So I ask myself:

Richard, is your diary wall-to-wall sport? Do you put the matches in before the more important responsibilities of church, family and friends?

The answers to those questions will help us realise whether we're fighting the desire for idolatry or whether we've simply surrendered to it. But we need to be warned. As with all idols, sport makes a useless saviour. It simply can't give us a life that will truly satisfy. It might make us happy in the short term. But it won't last.

It's only as we trust Christ as Saviour, follow Him as Lord and value Him as our treasure above everything else that we'll know true satisfaction and fulfilment. It's what we were made for and it's why He redeemed us. We may share in the temporary triumph of our team. But it won't save us or satisfy us. Our hearts will be restless until they find their rest in Him. His is the only victory to truly delight in. His triumph will capture our imagination and adoration for all eternity.

Not even an Ashes win Down Under does that!

Conclusion

Paul writes:

> So whether you eat or drink or whatever you do, do it all for the glory of God. **1 Corinthians 10 v 31**

Sport, like anything else in life, is an opportunity to draw attention to God's greatness. Wouldn't it be awesome if someone could see God glorified in the way I throw myself into enjoying sport—in front of the TV or at a live game?

Perhaps they'd spot me expressing my thanks to God for the sporting brilliance of the competitors, regardless of their nationality. Perhaps they'd see the level-headed way I coped with my team's victories and losses. Or perhaps they'd spot the way that I worshipped *Christ* as my heroic victor, not the guy who mounts the podium to take gold. I'd just love them to see me watching and enjoying sport to the full, but knowing at the same time that Christ and His gospel is what matters most.

A prayer

Thank You Heavenly Father for the gift of sport.
Thank You for the way it thrills me, and absorbs me.
Thank You for the joy of competition; the excitement of the game.
Please help me to enjoy it in a way that brings
    honour and glory to You.
Help me to respect all those who take part,
    and love what is good, true, noble and just.
And help me to rejoice more in the victory
    Your Son won for me on the cross.
Amen.

Further help

Idols, Julian Hardyman (IVP).
Don't waste your sports, C J Mahaney (Crossway).

Discuss

1. *What is your answer to these three questions:*
   - *Where does your mind go when you have nothing else to think about?*
   - *What's the subject of your most passionate conversations?*
   - *What do you put in your diary first that everything else has to fit around?*

   What do the answers tell you about what you truly worship?

2. **Read 1 Corinthians 10 v 31 again.**
   - *Think about what practical ways you can enjoy sport to the glory of God.*

   - *Think of one way you can show, or one thing you can say, to your friends, children, team mates, or opponents that will show that your true master is Jesus Christ.*

Martin: "The day the phone call came..."

I like football. Tennis is OK and athletics occasionally gets a look-in, but I'm a football man through and through.

I regularly finish off Saturday evening in front of the TV. I scour the internet for results and occasionally go to watch my team play. That's fine. As I said, I like football. It brings me pleasure. But it's not that important. Really, it's not.

But I used to *love* football—*really* love it. I'd slowly get up on a Saturday morning and grab the paper to read about the day's forthcoming games. My football knowledge levels suitably bolstered, I'd switch on the TV to watch some replays and analysis while I ate lunch.

Then if there was a home game on, I'd get on the bus and stand on the freezing terraces for two hours, screaming my lungs out at a group of players I thought I could identify with.

A few swear words would punctuate my shouts. Okay, I know it's hardly a good witness for a Christian, but in the heat of the moment, what can I say? After the game, it's back home for a tasty dinner and then out for the evening with a dissection or two of the day's games thrown in if I'm lucky.

Like I said, I used to love football. It gave me an energy and buzz that, to be frank, I rarely got from church, quiet times, prayer or Bible study. I know it's wrong and I'm not proud. It's even a little sad. Especially when the team you're so devoted to is Chesterfield.

So what changed? What brought God back to being my priority, my energy, my buzz, my life? I'd like to say that it was God ministering directly into my life, as the Bible pricked my conscience and prompted me to get my priorities straight. But it wasn't quite like that.

Amazingly, my little team got to the semi-finals of the FA Cup. I was there—on the second row at Old Trafford—shouting and singing for all I was worth. It was a fantastic game that ended 3-3 after extra time. The adrenaline pumped so hard that I was delirious, almost drunk on the excitement and unreality of the occasion.

A week later, it's the replay. This time I'm watching it on TV with a bunch of friends. The Blues get thrashed. They are unceremoniously dumped out of the cup. My dream is shattered. The depression hit immediately and, I'm ashamed to say, I probably drank a fair bit to compensate. I was low for days, really fed up.

Then the phonecall came. A good friend—someone

with a huge influence on me as a teenage Christian—had been diagnosed with terminal cancer. It hit me hard. But I knew that it wouldn't alter his love for Jesus and his determination to share the gospel with anyone who would listen. His football team would not be the focus of his conversations with unbelieving friends; Jesus would. I realised how stupid I had been to get so upset by the exploits of a football team. "Sorry Lord! I'm so obsessed by a game that I rarely talk to You or read Your word.

"I'm so fascinated by the results of a football team that I don't even notice that many of the people around me are heading towards eternal death. And I certainly don't tell them about You very often and about the incredible gift You have for them: Your own Son. How could I, when Liverpool have signed a Croatian striker?

"Sorry Lord. Help me to sort my priorities out. May I live for You and not football. May I talk to you every day and long to learn from Your awesome word. May I pluck up the courage to talk to my friends about You. Father, be my God again."

Yes, I still like football. I still check the scores and every now and then I'll slap down my money to shout at eleven men wearing the same colours as my scarf. But when we lose, I won't sulk. Well, not for more than an hour. You see, it's not important. It doesn't matter. It really is only a game. God my Father must have every place in my starting eleven.

T he man was breathing hard, but his eyes were focused and sharp. His body was numb with the effort he had been through. Every part of him hurt, but he kept repeating to himself: *"Just one more round to go"*.

He would never have made it this far had it not been for the guys in his corner. And especially the trainer. What he had said to him after the humiliating disaster of Round 8 had made all the difference.

"I'll let you into a secret," he had said. *"That guy has already lost. Disqualified from holding the title before he stepped in the ring. You don't have to knock him out. All you've got to do is get to the end, and you'll win."*

They had repeated it to him between every round since then. *"Just keep going—you can't lose if you just keep going."* But it had never been easy. There had been some tricky moments in every round. And the 13th had been particularly bad. The taunts, the jeering, and a low blow that the ref hadn't seen had sucked the willpower out of him. He'd slumped back on the stool, wanting to throw the towel in there and then.

But the team had been great. They were all seasoned fighters themselves, and they understood how hard it was out there on your own in the ring. They cautioned him again about keeping his guard up, but mostly it had been encouragement.

"Don't give up now. Think of the prize. Just keep going— you can't lose if you just keep going."

With ten seconds to go, he stood up, and stared across at the dark brooding presence sat in the opposite corner. He still looked terrifying, but now he seemed smaller, weaker.

It hardly seemed possible that he was still standing. A miracle really. And now the man had a deep confidence that he would get through. It wasn't a confidence born out of self belief. He had failed too many times in the previous rounds to know that.

No, it was a confidence rooted in knowing he was part of the winning team. He looked round at the guys in his corner, who were smiling at him now, and starting to clap their hands with joy. Just three more minutes of struggle, and then victory.

The noise rose to a new frenzy as the nasal tones of the announcer echoed around the great hall: "Seconds out, 15th and final round".

He stepped forward, braced for the final encounter as the bell rang...

Conclusion

We hope you have found the previous pages encouraging, stimulating and, in the right way, difficult. It's never easy to have your weaknesses and failures pointed out. It's always easier to go with the flow. It's always easier to give up and not struggle.

We hope that you have got the bigger picture of what resources we have been given for this fight. It's not a fight in which we are alone. The world, the flesh and the devil are powerful adversaries. But they will always be defeated when they meet their stronger counterparts: the fellowship of others, the internal empowerment of the Holy Spirit, and the Serpent Crusher Himself—the Lord Jesus Christ.

And it helps enormously to know that it's a fight that will one day end. The Bible closes with a glorious picture of all three enemies defeated. The devil and his minions are cast into hell. The unbelieving world, with all its false wealth and glory, is swept away by the judgment of God. And those who have been faithful are "made new", living for ever in the new creation, where there will be no more crying, grief or pain. A glorious peace after a lifetime of warfare.

All this helps, but in no way diminishes, the ferocity of the fight as we experience it sometimes. We're sorry if the particular thing you struggle with has not been specifically addressed in this book. But we pray that the general principles here will help you apply the gospel of God's grace to your heart and life. And we pray that you will use the resources God has given us so that, with the Apostle Paul, you are able to say: *"I have fought the good fight, I have finished the race, I have kept the faith"*.

Contributors

Trevor Archer (Grumbling) became the Director of Training for the UK Fellowship of Independent Evangelical Churches (FIEC) in January 2011, having retired from being the Senior Pastor at Chessington Evangelical Church since September 1986.

Paul Clarke (Gospelling) works on the staff team at St Helen's Church Bishopsgate, where he runs their small-group ministries and is the team leader for the Sunday morning congregation.

Richard Coekin (Guilt) is the Director of Co-Mission, a church-planting network in London, and the Senior Minister at Dundonald Church, Raynes Park, London.

Matt Fuller (Gold) is the Senior Minster at Christ Church Mayfair in central London, having been involved in this city-centre church since it was planted in 2001.

Mike McKinley (Gossip) is the Pastor of Guildford Baptist Church in Virginia, USA. He is a 9Marks blogger.

Wanyeki Mahiaini (Gifts) is the Associate Minister for Discipleship and Training at All Soul's Langham Place, London, UK.

Wes McNabb (Glare) is the Senior Pastor at Slade Evangelical Church, Plumstead, London.

Richard Perkins (Games) pastors Christ Church Balham, London and blogs at theurbanpastor.wordpress.com

Jason Roach (Girls) has recently planted The Bridge, a church reaching out to an inner-city area in Battersea, in partnership with the London City Mission.

Tim Thornborough (Grog) is the Editorial Director of the Good Book Company.

A Few Good Men
by Richard Coekin

A Few Good Men presents the reader with 10 positive role models from the Bible. From obedient Noah to loyal Onesiphorous, these character sketches combine dramatic story-telling with challenging and insightful comment. Solidly founded on biblical narrative, these chapters will challenge and inspire readers to examine the struggles and temptations of these biblical men who faced the same struggles that men still face today.

Men of God

Has there ever been a more urgent time for Christian men to stand up and be counted? This book is designed to encourage Christian men to live for Christ: in their homes; in their workplaces; in their leisure; and in their churches.

Contributions from John Benton, Richard Coekin, Phillip Jensen, David Jackman, Hugh Palmer, Vaughan Roberts, William Taylor, Rico Tice, John Tindall, Trevor Archer and Tim Thornborough.

Rock Solid: Men of Truth

Rock Solid aims to help us get to grips with Christian truth. If faith is not lived out, it is worth nothing. This book explains and clarifies twelve important and powerful doctrines, or "themes", from the Bible, so that we might have the comfort and assurance that comes from them, and so that we can make our life decisions by them. Ideal for groups to read so that they can get a clear hold on the truths that define who we are as followers of Christ.

Edited by Tim Thornborough & Trevor Archer

Man of God *10 studies*
by Sam Allberry and Anthony Bewes
This set of Bible studies aims to unpack the answers the Bible gives to the question of identity that men face today. We will learn our God-given role in creation, and how that has been ruined by the fall. And we will discover how we can start to be restored through the man above all men—Jesus Christ. Some things will be controversial in our culture. This course doesn't set out to be politically correct but faithful to God's counter-cultural word.

David: God's true king *6 studies*
by Nathan Buttery
We love David the hero, the shepherd boy who became king of Israel, chosen by God as a man "after His own heart". This Good Book Guide on the life of David reveals the secret of David's success and the reasons for his many failures. But it also uncovers the greater story of a better hero. You will learn how this weak King points us to the ultimate king— despised, rejected, yet finally winning the ultimate victory for His people over sin and death.

Work songs *6 studies by Tim Chester*
For many Christians there is a gap between church on Sunday and work on Monday. These songs encourage us to bridge that gap. They address the frustration we often feel with work, the temptations to compromise, the busyness and stress of the workplace and the sometimes overwhelming expectations of colleagues. They will also help us to celebrate the good days when everything goes like a dream.

Order from your friendly neighbourhood Good Book website:
UK & Europe: www.thegoodbook.co.uk • **N America:** www.thegoodbook.com
Australia: www.thegoodbook.com.au • **New Zealand:** www.thegoodbook.co.nz

thegoodbook
COMPANY
Opening up the Bible

At The Good Book Company, we are dedicated to helping individual Christians and local churches grow. We believe that God's growth process always starts with hearing clearly what He has said to us through His timeless word—the Bible.

Ever since we started in 1991, we have been striving to produce resources that honour God in the way the Bible is used. We have grown to become an international provider of user-friendly resources to the Christian community, with believers of all backgrounds and denominations using our Bible studies, books, evangelistic resources, DVD-based courses and training events.

We want to help equip ordinary Christians to live for Christ day by day, and churches to grow in their knowledge of God, their love for one another, and the effectiveness of their outreach. Call us to discuss your needs, or visit your friendly neighbourhood website for more information on the resources and services we provide.

UK & Europe: www.thegoodbook.co.uk
North America: www.thegoodbook.com
Australia: www.thegoodbook.com.au
New Zealand: www.thegoodbook.co.nz

UK & Europe: 0333 123 0880
North America: 866 244 2165
Australia: (02) 9564 3555
New Zealand: (+64) 3 343 1990

www.christianityexplored.org

Our partner site is a great place for those exploring the Christian faith, with a clear explanation of the good news, powerful testimonies and answers to difficult questions.

One life. What's it all about?

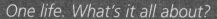